Haunted Encounters

Departed Family & Friends

Edited by Ginnie Siena Bivona and
Mitchel Whitington

Atriad Press • Dallas, Texas

Inquiries should be addressed to

Atriad Press
13820 Methuen Green
Dallas Texas, 75240
972-671-0002

www.atriadpress.com

Library of Congress Control Number 2005920906

International Standard Book Number 0-9740394-3-8

The editors wish to thank Alan McCuller for the outstanding cover art,
Martha McCuller for the beautiful interior design,
and Beth Kohler and Faye Voorhis for their excellent editorial work.
We are very grateful for their contributions.

All the events, persons, locations and organizations portrayed in this book are
based on true personal accounts experienced by the authors. Any resemblance to
any other experience is unintended and entirely coincidental.

1 3 5 7 9 8 6 4 2
Printed in the United States of America

Contents

Contents

Introduction

by Mitchel Whitington

I t is extremely difficult for many of us to contemplate death and the transition to the other side. Whether we call it "heaven," "nirvana," or simply the "spirit realm," it is only natural that we question what lies across that great chasm.

The question is magnified greatly when a loved one passes on. I remember losing a good friend, and as they were lowering his casket into the ground at the funeral, I couldn't help but think, "That's not him—that's not my buddy." He had merely shed his mortal body, as any of us might take off our work clothes at the end of the day. I knew that he was somewhere else right at that very moment, his spirit still very much alive, moving along on his journey.

No one knows what the other side is like, but as humans we feel compelled to find ways to describe it. As a youth, I was taught that it was a place where each of us would live in a huge mansion in a glorious city where the streets are literally paved with gold. Some world religions teach that those who die are taken to a massive party, with feasting and partaking in every pleasure that was forbidden them in their earthly lives. I once read a Hindu text describing the afterlife as a celestial garden, where "people of meritorious acts" wear garlands of flowers that never fade.

Because man is the only creature blessed/cursed with the ability to contemplate his own mortality, we each have to find some explanation that we can comfortably live with. At this stage of my life, one of the best descriptions of heaven for me was offered by Mitch Albom in his book, *The Five People You Meet in Heaven*. Although it is a fictitious tale, I found it comforting. I'll probably carry it in my mind until the appointed time to make the journey myself.

It also helps when I'm thinking about friends and family who have departed this world. When I envision my Granddad, I can close my eyes and see him bass fishing on a mountain lake where there are no daily limits, no game wardens, and the only reason that the fish stop biting is to give him a chance to change lures for a little variety.

A friend of mine is busy whistling a tune as he builds fences around a massive, lush, green pasture so to raise a prize herd of cattle—one of his favorite activities when he was here on Earth. His dogs, who both went on before him, have probably found him and are romping at his feet and chasing an occasional rabbit across the field.

Yet another friend is racing his car along country roads at speeds that, were I with him, would make me close my eyes in terror, just as I did when he was alive. Now my pal is shifting gears and zooming along without any speed limits, stop signs, or highway patrol officers.

These are simply my own visions, ones that I've conjured up for lack of a better understanding of the afterlife.

Occasionally, some of us on this side do get a chance for an actual peek into that other world when a departed friend or family member comes back for a brief visit. As I read the stories in this book, I found many wonderful tales of such occurrences. I discovered the spirit of a man who sends the sign of a bird to his best friend whenever she needs him most. I smiled at a delightful story about a loving father who crosses the boundary of death to return to his daughter's house, and play his favorite old song on her stereo—just to let her know that he's watching over her. One of the most touching was a tale of a woman whose mother returned for a single visit, just to say "I'm all right; everything is beautiful here." Reading these true encounters was an emotional experience for me. More than a few brought a tear to my eye, and some made me laugh out loud.

I sometimes wonder why, with all of the supernatural experiences that I've had, I've never had a visit from one of the family or friends that I've lost over the years. It's only a fleeting thought, though. I know that they're all off on their own journeys, and if the need ever arises, they would gladly make that crossing, just like the spirits in this book did. Right now, though, the memories of my departed family and friends are enough, and I'm content to read these wonderful experiences. Besides, I'd hate to interrupt a single moment of Granddad's fishing.

Mitch Whitington
Senior Editor, Atriad Press LLC

I Sing of the Burlaps Electric

by Nan B. Clark

We called them the Burlap Sisters in a parody of the era in which they grew up, the Big Band and swing era, a time of saddle shoes and bobbysocks, of barrettes and poodle skirts, of the Andrews Sisters and the Clooney Sisters snapping their fingers and harmonizing into microphones the size of breadboxes.

Despite the fact that they had grown up on a farm in Derry, New Hampshire—hence the burlap—my mother, Annie, and her sister, Gen, were bee-bopping, cool-jive chicks, both graduates of a secretarial school in New York City right after World War II. The world was not only raining men, it was positively drowning in them—GIs back from the trenches and ready to celebrate life.

Smoking? It was great for the figure! Drinking? It was great for the soul! And tooling around in a shiny, black, beetle-bumpered Buick was the cat's meow!

Annie and Gen eventually settled down just as Ike and Mamie moved into the White House and the world started thinking collectively about what nastiness to indulge in next. Nukes won out and by the time my cousins and I were born, the mushroom-shaped cloud dominated our nightmares.

Nightmares about World War III or not, we all grew up—my sister and I and my two cousins, Gen's son and daughter—in happy homes. The 1950s really were a time for baking cookies

1

and "flying up" in scout troops. The 1960s saw us heading off for college, and, in one case, Vietnam. Happily, we all survived. Family reunions, complete with lots of liquor and laughter, were the norm.

Annie died in a nursing home in the early hours of Saturday, February 10, 2001, after a long bout with osteoporosis. That afternoon, my sister and I and our husbands went to the bar of a lovely country inn in Derry, New Hampshire, having completed the funeral arrangements just as Annie wanted. The four of us moved in a haze of grief and exhaustion, but the inch or so of brandy in the snifters was enough to cheer us as we sank onto the comfortable sofas pulled up to the gas-fired logs in the fireplace.

Just as we were starting to relax, a tremendous clamor broke out. Something had set off the fire alarm. Too numb to move, we watched as the few diners in the place at that odd time headed for the door, followed by the kitchen staff. Everyone stampeded by us but nobody stopped to ask, "What are you, deaf? Get up! Get out!"

Sipping our brandy, we sat in the tremendous, ear-splitting squall of the alarm until, just a few minutes later, a squad of firefighters trooped in. Again, they walked by us as if we were invisible, and stormed into the kitchen. After a moment, the hideous clamor stopped. There wasn't the slightest trace of fire or smoke. Electrical problem, the firefighters said, and left.

"I apologize for the disruption," the manager said when he came back into the bar, his face red from more than the bitter cold. "This has never happened before."

He felt the need to reassure us, as we had booked the upstairs room for an expensive luncheon after the funeral service the following Monday. "No problem," we said, and finished our drinks.

In the car, the four of us all said aloud what we had been thinking. Annie! All that energy—it had to have gone somewhere. "And if anybody would pull off one last practical joke, it was Mum," my sister and I agreed, laughing at the thought that she couldn't bear to be left out of any party.

Of course, Gen and her family were at the funeral, still cracking jokes as Annie lay in her coffin looking eerily like a teenager. After the service, we watched in silence as the funeral director cranked the pillow down, folded the soft material around her smiling face, and finally lowered the lid. Our grown children seized the handles and carried her to the hearse for the short trip to the family plot in the ancient graveyard just up the street.

By the time the immediate family got back from the gravesite, the party at the inn was in full swing. We sat with our loved ones, eating delicious food, drinking wine, and toasting Annie wistfully. Just as we were finishing dessert, a hideous but familiar clamor filled the place.

"Fire!" Our guests pushed back their chairs and started to head for the door.

"Wait a minute," we said, but the damage was done. Down went Annie's guests, throwing on their coats as they flew outdoors into the icy sunshine.

This time Gen's family stayed with us on the second floor as, shouting over the alarm, we told them we thought it was Annie saying good-bye.

Again.

And again, the alarm finally stopped and the manager appeared, filled with worried apologies.

What had actually gone on in that old inn? We don't know, but what we do know is that less than a month later, the place went up for sale, changed hands, and became a Tex-Mex place.

Now that would have been just an amusing family story if another jolt hadn't been delivered one year later, when Gen died after failing to recover from a hip replacement. Many things were the same—the quick and merciful death in a nursing home, the raw time of year when the branches were bare and even the sunshine bore no warmth.

Coming home from the nursing home immediately after her death, my uncle and his son entered the silent house to begin the miserable task of calling people. Just as he picked up the phone, my aunt's husband of more than half a century heard a tremendous clamor in his garage, where Gen's car had been parked for weeks.

Rushing into the freezing dusk, my cousin and my uncle opened the garage door to see her car flicking its lights and beeping for all it was worth. By the time my uncle got the car door unlocked, the garage had fallen silent and the lights had gone out.

"The Burlap Sisters, together at last," the handful of us who shared the strange events agreed. We hope we can go out with such merry energy when our time comes too.

Nan Clark's interest in the otherworldly includes a lifelong fascination with the long-dead Hawthornes, not just Nathaniel but especially his sister Elizabeth, who lived for thirty years in one room of an old colonial home a quarter of a mile away from Nan's in Beverly, Massachusetts.

Uncle Leo's Pennies

by Diane Murphy

All who live in my house and those who visit will find pennies—here, there, pennies everywhere! From heaven? Perhaps. I call them "Uncle Leos."

If ever there was a charmer with a rich, infectious, fat, and raspy laugh, it was dear Uncle Leo, an insurance salesman, one of my mother's four siblings, and one of my favorite relatives. Although the man, a World War II veteran, exhibited traits of bravado at times, he was mostly mild-mannered, a smile-on-the-sleeve kind of guy who met everyone with a twinkle in his eye.

You never knew what he was up to. A prankster in his own right, the eyebrow-raising Jack Nicholson-look-alike and grandiose master storyteller could captivate you while he effortlessly embroidered a sad sack anecdote, the sort of tale that brings you to tears, only to arrive at the epilogue with a big "did I get ya good?" finish. He was a scream!

He touched my life many times with kind words and gestures when I needed it the most, especially on one specific occasion when I was a girl of seventeen. I had a difficult decision to make. All was not well at home, to say the least, and despite the unrest between my parents, the dear man would never think of taking sides. He loved his sister dearly. He and my father were good pals. Everyone in the family was aware of the ongoing unsettling problems. Out of respect and perhaps even more out of kindness, it was never brought out into the open at any family gathering. If there were whispers, my older sister and I were spared from hearing a word. Nevertheless, I was making plans to move out to save my sanity.

On my cousin Nathan's wedding day, Uncle Leo waited for me to arrive at the church for his son's wedding and greeted me with open arms as he delicately pulled me aside on the steps. While holding my hand, he said in his loving, discreet tone: "Your aunt and I have heard of your recent plans. We understand. Just know we approve of this decision. It is the right one. We wanted you to know that." This was a great gift, one I treasure.

He always made me feel as though he had a protective wing over me. His visits to our house, or ours to his, were not that frequent but always happy.

A few years later, it was my turn to get married. I was leaving Montréal and all my beloved ones to move to Halifax, Nova Scotia, with my husband.

I had a busy life. I was a young married woman in my twenties and a working mother raising a son and daughter. I was making the best out of being so far away from everybody. Although I kept in touch with all my relatives, it had never crossed my mind that one day I would pick up that phone and at the other end of the line would be those awful words uttered by one of them, the kind that make you reel so much with pain you can't scream out when they say someone in your family has died.

Uncle Leo had passed away. Somehow, my immediate family had waited too long to get in touch with me and I was unable to fly home in time for the funeral.

It felt as though I had let him down and he had abandoned me until the dreams began. Uncle Leo came into my dreams for almost two years, on a regular basis. I remember some of those dreams vividly; others have faded. Then, one day, I suppose he decided it was time to change his style and really show off a little with a different kind of contact.

I was expecting my third child. The crib was next to our bed. It was all made up with a pretty little sheet, receiving blanket, pillow, and plush toys, even a mobile hanging over it. I knew the day was near. I was filled with excitement, just knowing I would finally be meeting and holding my infant in a matter of days, if not hours. The anticipation of being able to bend forward, not to mention the out-of-reach privilege of seeing and grabbing my toes again, was nothing less than outstanding. Although I couldn't put my finger on it, something else was stirring within me, a state I can only describe as a child-like lighthearted gladness.

A day before my baby girl decided she was going to announce her arrival into this world, the first of many spirit manifestations from my uncle began. It was midmorning and my husband, Dan, should have already left the house for the office. I had slept in, and I woke up trying to let go of a dream in which Uncle Leo was saying, as I recall, he could not return for a while. As I was trying to open my eyes, I noticed there was a trail of smoke going out into the hallway at the other end of the room while the bedroom door was slowly being closed. That door was always left open. I could also smell the distinct odor of a freshly lit cigarette. I was a little startled. I stumbled out of bed and called out to see if Dan was in the house, I thought he had perhaps left late for work or come back because he had forgotten something, but I was especially wondering if he had started smoking again. I knew I wasn't imagining things.

There definitely had been someone in my room. After checking out the house and realizing nobody else was home, I called Dan at the office and, sure enough, he answered, so he couldn't have just left. I told him what was going on about the cigarette smoke and the door closing slowly. His reaction was a little patronizing as he went on to say I must have been half asleep. He suggested I go back under the blankets, rest, and take it easy. As for going back to smoking again, he totally denied it before saying good-bye. When I hung up the phone, I noticed there was no smoke or smell of cigarettes. It had vanished into thin air. What I had seen was real. I knew it wasn't my imagination. The evening hours would prove it.

That same night, when it was time to retire, the two little ones were fast asleep and so was my Dan. Moonlight was shining through the window, on a penny lying on the carpet on my side of the bed. I thought this was a little odd. Where could this have come from? I kept a tight ship. Too lazy to pick it up, I left it there. It's not like it was going anywhere—or so I thought. It was on the carpet, right next to the crib.

As I started to doze off, I heard this little noise, as if something light had been thrown on the crib's rigid mattress. Even sounded as if it had bounced. Out of curiosity, I rolled out of bed to see what this could be. A fallen toy from the mobile maybe? No, it wasn't that at all. That penny I hadn't picked up off the carpet was now right smack in the middle of the baby's crib.

I wanted to wake up Dan to tell him but decided not to, although I would change my mind just a few minutes later when my water broke. It was show time! Dear funny Uncle Leo had flicked that penny up there. No doubt in my mind. The gent was quite the smoker and the life of the party. There was about to be a celebration in my life and he wanted me to know he was there. I believed it with all my heart.

There's more to this affinity.

Although the dreams stopped for a while, he did come back in flashes, making cameo appearances. I remember the night of our last encounter during my sleep. He told me to let him go once and for all and that he could not come anymore. I was terribly sad and felt as though I'd been scolded but I was also upset, thinking I might have kept him from other matters in his realm, and so it ended but not altogether.

On occasion, I did, and still do, smell but not see the cigarette smoke, and so does my family. But there's something else he's left with me—a token of his affection. In any house I've lived in since, we find pennies galore! They are everywhere, all the time. I have jars and little coin dishes full of Uncle Leo pennies. Not only does he drop them at will but he helps us find lost things in the house with them.

One day as I was frantically looking for my purse, I saw a penny on the floor so I decided to talk to my uncle, hoping he would be listening, and asked him if he could help me. I asked if I would toss the penny and watch where it landed, if it would lead me to my purse. On my second or third try, I watched the penny land near a chair with a ruffle that touched the floor. I looked around and underneath the chair. There was my purse.

My uncle manifested his presence in spirit in my house for the first time in 1979 and is still often with us. We don't need to toss the pennies around anymore. All we do is ask him and we find whatever has been misplaced (or hidden by the cats or other entities, as I can assure you we do not live alone). We've told this story to family and friends alike who have adopted this relative of mine. He also seems to be more than willing to help out in the lost-and-found area whenever he can.

He must have passed the word on because I'm being nickel-and-dimed by other relatives beyond—my godmother, Aunt Evelyn, she with the nickels, and my Uncle Stony, he with the dimes. They've both passed on in recent years.

Over and above the distinct smells that bring the memory of departed ones to mind—perfume, a pot of Italian sauce brewing (when all we're having is salad), etc.—Uncle Leo has become a go-between of sorts, warning me of the coming passing of a family member, one about to leave for the hereafter. I receive blank—completely blank—and unidentified faxes, source unknown with the fax caller ID function not displaying. It is always one single sheet, totally white. It has been five years since I've last received such a message. When my fax rings unexpectedly in the wee hours of the night, I hope and pray it's just some telemarketing annoyance and nothing else.

A toast to Uncle Leo and to all of you who have read his story so graciously!

––––––––

Diane Murphy grew up in Montréal, Québec, in a household where French and English were spoken fluently, with a dash of Italian on occasion. Her mother, who hailed from North Adams, Massachusetts, was an exquisite artist. It wasn't unusual for Diane to come to the breakfast table for some cereal with a side order of Mom's sketches or the new lyrics to a song she'd created during the night, but it was their talks about nightly dreams that were the best. Diane landed her first exciting job in the motion picture industry where she was involved in film rental, along with writing and translating promotional copy. After she married, her husband's career took them to Halifax where all three of their children were born. Ten years later they were transferred to Toronto and Diane began a new business venture as a freelance creative specialist. She still likes to write about movies but she truly has a passion for expressing her unusual experiences, in and out of dreams. She can be reached at finalwordtranslation@yahoo.ca.

Grandma

by Melissa Mathis

My parents had been born and raised up north, but when I was about three years old they packed us up and moved us out east to get away from the cold and snow. As a result, I grew up without grandparents or aunts and uncles around. To make up for this, my parents would send me "back home" every summer to stay with my grandma and grandpa.

I loved the change of pace from the bustling city to the slow summers in the country. I spent those long warm days running through vast grassy fields and shady green forests filled with wildflowers and raspberry patches. Getting scratched by thorn bushes and dodging honeybees while trying to get to the plumpest, reddest berries was my idea of heavenly pleasure.

My grandmother, although she did not have any formal education in either subject, was an avid science and nature fan, so much so that she said she was going to donate her body to science when she died. She always told me that if she could have her way she would like to be one of the skeletons that are hung in medical schools.

She exposed me to her wonder of science and nature by taking me on long walks on those dewy summer mornings to gather various insects to study. We would collect cocoons for moths and butterflies, keeping them in jars. To my fascination, weeks later, they would open, revealing what my grandma called "their secrets." I was always surprised to discover something popping out of those little cocoons, whether a colorful butterfly or a dusty gray moth.

Grandma borrowed old moldy science books from the local library. We used them to study all of the parts from the dead beetles and cicada shells we found, naming all of the little hairy legs and wings. Grandpa would bring home the catch from his afternoon spent at the lake fishing, and Grandma and I would dissect the fish and study their insides before she cleaned them for dinner.

In this way and in so many others my grandmother was influential in my life. It was a great delight to her when she heard that I had decided to major in medicine in college.

But, heartbreakingly, at the beginning of my first year of med school my grandmother passed away. True to her word, she donated her body to science, which was taken straight from the hospital, leaving us with no body to bury and no closure or chance to say good-bye. I jumped back into my studies full force after her death with an even stronger desire to make her proud of me.

A couple of months after her death, I was in my little studio apartment writing a paper for a class that I was having a particularly hard time with. I had been going at it all morning and into the afternoon. I was about three-quarters finished with the paper and was stuck. I was absolutely stumped as to how to tie it all up and finish the paper. Filled with frustration, I collapsed on my bed in tears and fell asleep. I was awakened by something sharp poking me. The room was completely dark but for the light coming from the computer monitor.

I went and turned on the light so I could get a better look at what poked me. It was the corner of an old reference book that I hadn't used or looked at in ages. It was lying there open to the middle, halfway protruding from under my blue and red comforter. Looking at the book, I noticed that it was open to the exact topic that my paper was on! I read through the first couple of paragraphs with growing excitement. It completely opened my eyes as to how to finish my paper. I didn't think too much at the time about how the book had gotten there. But later, when I went to put it back, I realized that this book had been in a box under my bed for well over a year.

Several weeks later were midterms. I was in class taking one of my tests and was having trouble with a particular section of questions on anatomy. I skipped over the questions, hoping when I came back to them the answers would come to me. I completed the rest of the test with ease, yet was still so confused that I could not finish. I had a mental block and time was ticking. I sat staring at my desk, then the clock, counting the seconds. Panic set in as I saw other students turning in their papers and leaving. I started calculating the percentage I would get if I did not answer these questions and knew that I would not pass the exam unless I answered them.

By now, I was the last person left. I looked up at the clock and saw that there were only twenty minutes left for me to finish my test. I was growing angrier with every passing moment. I was ready to randomly guess the answers to the questions when I noticed the skeleton in the front of the room. It was usually facing outward when not in use, but now it was turned at such an odd angle that I instinctually followed its "gaze" and there it was—a diagram of the anatomy of the human body.

Somehow just seeing that diagram made everything make sense. It clicked! The answers came flooding to me, and suddenly I could not write fast enough. I finished the test with all the confidence in the world that I had passed. When I completed the questions and looked back up, the skeleton was facing forward again. I looked around to see if anyone had moved it, but I was the last person left in the class and the professor was busy at his desk going through the finished exams. I turned in my paper and left the classroom with an eerie sense of wonder. Was my grandma reaching out to me from the other side?

During the winter break from school, I decided to go back to my grandparents' home for a visit. I had a great time visiting with my grandpa but my main reason was to see if I could feel my grandmother's spirit and get some answers about the strange events I had been experiencing. I had expected to feel her presence or to notice things move while I wasn't looking. Nothing at all happened throughout my stay. I even prodded my grandfather with veiled questions to see if he had noticed anything strange. If he did, he wasn't admitting it.

By the end of my break I had dismissed the whole idea of my grandmother's spirit trying to get in touch with me as just a figment of my studied-out and overstressed imagination.

After the holidays I went back to school refreshed and ready to jump back into my studies with renewed enthusiasm. My second week back in class we had just gotten our first human cadavers to dissect. Due to other students' exuberance I tended to get pushed to the back. Luckily, my professor had noticed this. He was nice enough to offer to spend extra time with me after class. He would allow me to work at my own pace, overcoming some of my intimidation from cutting a real person. It was during this time that my grandmother left no doubts in my mind that she was still a very real and active part of my life.

The following week, while in an after-class session, the professor said he was going to run down to the lounge to grab a cup of coffee. He would be right back. While he was gone I decided to go over to the cadaver just to get my courage up a little. Standing over the body with the scalpel in my grasp, I felt a hand on my shoulder. I stayed focused on the cadaver, thinking the professor had come back and was giving me an encouraging pat on the back. Meanwhile, all of my fear and intimidation melted away and a serene calm came over me.

I had the peaceful feeling of those long summer days spent in the kitchen with my grandma cutting open the fish that my grandpa brought home for dinner. Before I knew it I was handling the scalpel like a pro, and after making the first couple of cuts I finally looked up and realized that I was still alone in the room. The professor hadn't come back yet. I looked toward the front of the classroom and noticed the skeleton in the corner swinging gently as if someone had just put it back on its hook.

Just then the professor walked in with his coffee in one hand. When he saw what I had done, he got a big smile on his face. Like a father watching an infant take those first steps, he radiated pride. I smiled back, knowing that with the support I had, I could not fail.

I am through with school now and onto my rotations. I don't feel my grandma's presence as often now. Only in particularly stressful situations and only when it involves medicine will I feel that hand on my back. A peaceful calm will come over me and I get a big smile on my face knowing that I am loved and watched out for.

Melissa Mathis currently resides in Tucson, Arizona, a city surrounded by mountains and filled with cultural diversity. In Tucson, you can dine at some of the finest resorts in the United States or eat Mexican food wrapped in paper from a stand on the side of the road. Melissa takes full advantage of the uniqueness of the town, which allows her to experience the best from both ends of the spectrum.

She also loves to travel and has done so extensively throughout her childhood and into her adult life. She thrives on meeting new people and seeing new places. This has seasoned her writing with an insight and sophistication well beyond her twenty-nine years.

Autumn's Spirit

by Kriss Erickson

When my mother was in the final stages of her battle with cancer, she insisted that I take a rare break from caring for her to enjoy the beauty and color of the New England autumn. Autumn was her favorite season. Instead of seeing it as the season before winter's deadness, she saw autumn as a time of fulfillment. She loved the crisp air and the gorgeous colors of the changing leaves. She often said that she felt more alive during autumn than at any other time of the year.

As I drove through the rounded hills that rambled through our small New Jersey town and spread upward, though New York State and into Canada, I gasped at the brilliance of autumn's fireworks. The scenery was more lively and chaotic than a Fourth of July celebration.

When I reached a quiet northern New Jersey town, I pulled over on a tree-lined street. I walked past shops selling fresh cider, pumpkin pies, and beeswax candles, delighting in the crunch-crunch of the dry brown leaves beneath my sneakers. As I breathed a great gulp of the brisk air, my lungs filled with energy. The brilliant reds, golds, and oranges of the changing leaves simultaneously made my eyes smart and embraced me in the grand dignity of mature life.

It felt as if the leaves were using their bright colors to proclaim their determination to celebrate each moment of life, even through their last burst of energy. The autumn wind tugged my denim skirt. I decided to use the wind as a rudder in this sea of fall's glory. I obeyed the tugging wind, following the blowing leaves. I window shopped, letting the spirit of autumn choose my path.

The wind and leaves led me to a small shop that contained a large display of porcelain statues of the wild birds that frequented the New England area. The birds were crafted so delicately that they looked alive. My mother loved birds, especially bluebirds. Since she couldn't be with me to enjoy this marvelous autumn day, I bought her a delicate rendering of a bluebird perched on a dogwood branch. The bird looked skyward, its wings slightly spread, as if preparing to take flight.

"This bird is just like my mother," I thought. "She's getting ready to fly away, too."

Though I didn't want her to leave, I knew that we all follow the seasons of our lives. As I walked back to my car, I collected a bouquet of leaves with the greatest variety of colors and shapes that I could find. Yellow aspen, knobby red oak, pointy, florid maple, orange elm, slender golden willow—they made as colorful an arrangement as a bouquet of flowers.

I wondered if my mother knew that this would be her last opportunity to enjoy the spectacular autumn display. She hadn't been strong enough to get out of bed since July. A sudden gust of wind ruffled my hair. That was my mother's special greeting. I turned into the wind, swallowing a huge, painful lump in my throat. I hoped the statue and leaf bouquet would help her to be a part of this day.

As I opened the car door, the bluebird statue seemed to leap from my hands. It fell onto the pavement, breaking in two. When I picked it up I noticed that the body of the bluebird was hollow inside. I started to walk back to the store, to return it, but felt compelled to keep the damaged statue. I wondered if the spirit of the bird, like my mother's spirit, had yearned to break free. Suddenly, I felt alone, as if a presence had vacated this perfect fall day.

When I returned home two hours later, the coroner's van was parked in front of our house. My hands went numb, my carefully gathered leaf bouquet scattered across the ground as I ran up our front steps.

"I'm sorry," my father said when I met him in the living room. "Your mother died about two hours ago. It was the strangest thing," he mused, wiping a handkerchief across his reddened eyes. "She asked me to open the curtains this morning, so she could see the leaves on the maple trees in our front yard. The last thing she said, was 'Look! A bluebird.' We've never had bluebirds here. But I'm sure she saw one."

"I'm sure she did, too," I answered, tears pouring down my face.

I thought of the wonderful day I'd spent in autumn's splendor. Now the beckoning trees, the hair-ruffling wind, the leaf bouquet, and the broken bluebird statue made sense.

I hadn't enjoyed the splendor of autumn by myself that day, after all. My mother's spirit had gone with me. She'd spent the day with me, until it was time for her spirit to break free. Now she was free, like the bluebird's spirit, merging with the outlandish fall colors, riding the autumn winds.

After we'd made the funeral arrangements, I gathered my leaf bouquet and scattered it around a collage of family pictures. I placed the porcelain statue of the bluebird beside the picture frame, carefully balancing the bird's broken body on the dogwood stem.

"That's a pretty statue," my father commented. "Aren't you going to repair it?"

I shook my head.

"I bought this statue for Mom. I think it broke the moment she died. Look."

I lifted the bird's hollow body so he could see inside.

"Its spirit escaped, just like hers. Maybe, if I leave the bird as it is, she'll have a place to come and rest."

"I hope so," he said, patting my shoulder.

I don't know for sure if my mother's spirit used the porcelain bluebird's hollow center as a place of rest. But the corner where it sat, surrounded by the dried leaves of the last autumn day that we spent together, always seemed warmer than the rest of the house. And sometimes, when I dusted the picture frame, a gentle wind ruffled my hair. Its touch felt just like my mother's fingers.

Kriss Erickson is a versatile freelance writer with over three hundred stories, articles, recipes, and books published since she began writing professionally in 1981. Since that time, she has contributed stories and articles for over seventy-five magazines. Her cookbook *Healthy Gourmet Cheesecakes: Simple Recipes for Sensational Cheesecakes* was published in 1998 by Avery Publishing (ISBN 0-89529-783-3). Kriss won fourth place in 2000 in PublishingOnline's fiction contest for her young adult fantasy novel *The Land Behind the Veil: Book I.*

Kriss completed a master of arts in counseling and a certificate in spiritual direction in 2003. She lives in Everett, Washington, on a ¾-acre wetland and bird sanctuary with her husband, Michael, and her nine-year-old son, Jason. Visit Kriss's web site at http://slverkriss.tripod.com or e-mail her at slverkriss@aol.com.

The Love Lives On

by Sylvia M. DeSantis

 om thinks a moment before taking a sip, squinting through the steam rising from her coffee cup as she holds it to her lips.

"We can't really mention this to anyone. People will think I should be put away!"

Because I try to understand and cherish our experiences with paranormal phenomenon, I bristle at the idea of someone, anyone, disbelieving my mother or insinuating that she's crazy for speaking of her experience. But realistically, I know she's right. In our traditional Italian Catholic family, chatting about ghostly encounters isn't really considered acceptable. But that doesn't mean Mom and I haven't had our share of experiences. I feel bad for Mom. She's clearly a little shaky this morning. The night before had been a long one.

Mom had called me earlier than usual, catching me at my desk just as I had begun grading essays and answering my e-mail.

"Could you maybe come home this weekend?"

"Mom? Is something wrong?" I know my mother well enough to recognize the funny catch in her voice that signals some problem.

"No, I'm fine. I just had… a strange experience last night. Well, actually I think I might have had, I don't know, a seizure…."

At this piece of news I begin packing up for the day and turning students away although I've just begun office hours. I cut her off before she can finish.

"I'll be there in three hours."

"Well," shrugs Mom as we talk, "I've been dreaming of Nana and Poppy a lot lately. Maybe they're watching over me."

I sit with eyes wide, unsure how to respond to my mom's story. I shouldn't be so surprised since Mom and I have been "tuned in" to alternative energies for years. We always knew when the other was calling on the phone long before caller ID made its debut, and we both feel we've been visited in different ways by my sister, who passed away over twenty years ago.

Having a second sense and being "visited" had been natural to both of us for most of our lives, but not until I was older did I realize that we could talk about these abilities and experiences as something special between us, a precious gift. But this story—the seizure and the ghostly visitation—isn't our usual simple prescience. When she tells me how it all happened, how she felt during the night, and how she knows she is being watched and cared for, I feel tears come to my eyes.

Mom explains how the intense rattling in her chest began a little after midnight. Full from snacks, she had skipped dinner and gone to bed without eating for over seven hours, a reckless mistake for any diabetic but especially dangerous for someone with my mother's blood sugar history. When the shaking began, Mom knew immediately that she was in trouble. The seizing became stronger and stronger as her body grew more and more rigid.

"My God," she says, "I was alone in the house, having a seizure that paralyzed me. I was terrified in a way I have never experienced before in my life."

Her paralyzed body jerked uncontrollably, throwing itself across the bed, knocking over her bedside water glass, and kicking sheets, blankets, and a small lamp to the floor.

"This wasn't just a chill. I couldn't move and my body was being shaken from the inside out. My teeth literally rattled in my mouth and my ribs hurt horribly from the force of being jerked so hard. The entire time my mind was incredibly clear. I actually thought my bones would break because I was thrashing so hard.

"I felt death near to me and had the very clear thought that I would die. I felt a jolt of horror when I realized that either you or your brother would find me dead. I didn't know how I could forgive myself for that.

"A warm calm swept across my body, as though I'd been wrapped in a blanket of love and peace. The feeling erased all of the pain I'd ever felt in my life and I've lived a long time! I didn't know what to think."

Although her limbs were still paralyzed, Mom managed to open her eyes and turn her head slightly to the left, where the vision awaiting her nearly took her breath away again.

Within a hazy cloud of whitish-blue surrounding the bed and hovering over Mom was her mother, our Nana, who passed away in 1995. Nana swept along and over Mom, gently pulling the blankets back up and across her body. As the seizure slowed to a slight tremble, Mom's frozen limbs began to relax. Mom closed her eyes tightly, unsure of what she had seen, and felt the lightest touch on her face, a soft hand brushing her hair from her eyes and stroking her forehead gently. She opened her eyes once more, determined to remember the moment, trying desperately to absorb the expression on her mother's face, a face she hadn't seen in over five years.

"'This is a miracle,' I kept saying to myself. What else could it be other than that? I've never done drugs and this was no dream.

I know what it was! This visit was a gift from my mother who stills watches over me even though I'm an old woman myself!"

As Mom began to roll over, still barely comprehending what had just happened, a dark shape caught her attention.

"There, at the foot of the bed, stood my father. My father! He wore a formal suit and looked wonderful and strong, with a full head of his bright red hair. I remember that hair so well from childhood. Although I haven't seen him with so much hair since he was a young man and we were children, I would recognize that crazy shock of red anywhere!"

Poppy stood by the bed calmly, watching silently. Suddenly, Nana was next to Poppy, standing quietly, waiting for the last of the shakes to leave Mom's body. As soon as her breathing slowed and the shaking completely stopped, they were both gone, slowly fading away along with the beautiful bluish glow that had been enveloping the bed.

"It was unbelievable, absolutely crazy. My mother and my father, at my bedside, saving me from a diabetic seizure! This is not something I'll be sharing with Dr. B—at my next visit."

As Mom recounts her story, sheepishly hiding behind her coffee cup but nodding knowingly, her face clouds and she tries not to cry. I watch her struggle to make sense of it all—the seizure, death so close, the visitation by her parents, the whole scary and miraculous evening.

"I've been blessed. And now I know that my time here isn't yet over. People can say what they want about this story, but I'll always know and believe. That's the gift my parents gave to me—the miracle of their visit. They gave me back life."

An English and women's studies instructor who now designs educational multimedia, Sylvia M. DeSantis lives with her partner in State College, Pennsylvania, where she writes poetry, fiction, and essays, and works with the natural healing arts. Esoteric encounters and strong prescience have "haunted" Sylvia her whole life but have become especially pronounced since she began healing work with Usui Reiki in 2001. Sylvia is the August 2004 "Somewhere In America Short, Short Fiction" contest winner and a contributor to Greenwood Publishing's forthcoming *The Encyclopedia of Multiculturalism*. She has recently placed a poem in Inglis House's 2004 *Dancing With Cecil* chapbook. Writing for *Haunted Encounters* has helped Sylvia find balance in her writing life, bringing it full circle by giving voice to the encounters she and her mother, Maria, have experienced for many years.

Reconciled

by Thomas Humphrey

My wife, Alicia, and I were divorced in 1998. Although, as with any divorce, there was much acrimony during the ordeal, we learned to forgive each other and became close a year or so after the decree was entered. Consequently, I was devastated when, in the early fall of 2000, she unexpectedly passed away. What was worse, I did not learn of her passing until over a month later, missing the funeral, the traditional time and place to say good-bye.

She had moved back home after the divorce, several hundred miles away, and her family, unlike Alicia, still held animosity toward me, and almost unforgivably, chose not to tell me of her death. I learned of it through a friend. It left me numb, and the nature of how I received the news left me almost in disbelief.

A couple of months went by. Then one night as I lay in bed, I had this odd sensation—at least odd to me—that Alicia was trying to talk to me. I felt, rather than really heard, her voice, trying to tell me something, I could not tell what, but I sensed somehow she was trying to communicate with me. I shrugged it off. While I was not completely opposed to any notion that the dead could communicate with those of us still on earth, I was less convinced that any of them, no matter how close they were to me, would try to talk to me or that I even had the ability to hear them.

Over two years went by and I still could not come to terms with Alicia's passing. It was hard for me even to believe sometimes that she was gone. One evening, a young girl whom I had befriended was staying at my house. There was nothing romantic between us and, in fact, she was staying with me while she sorted out her own personal problems.

Corindee was one of those troubled young people who, it seems, had emotions that were not keeping up with her intellect. She was bright and wise beyond her years but continued to find herself in difficult spots where her emotional needs had put her.

This particular evening, Corindee was playing on my computer in my home office while I sat across my desk—fiddling with paperwork I think—while we chatted.

I had not discussed my ex-wife with her or anyone else who did not know Alicia. It was a topic I struggled with. Unless prodded, I did not speak of good times, bad times—anything. It was a part of my life that I kept to myself. When she somehow brought up the subject of prior marriages, I told her the full story. Corindee was amazed at this new information but, after I explained the reason behind my silence, something I did not even realize myself until that moment, she seemed to understand.

We sat quietly for a few moments, the topic having lent itself to a break in conversation before we could move on to another. Suddenly, Corindee perked up, straightening in her chair.

"Does your sister have a dog, Tom?" she said.

I was puzzled. Before I could answer, she asked, "Did your ex-wife have a dog?"

She did indeed have a dog. Alicia was as much of a dog lover as I am. I said, "Yeah," with a pause, and then "Why?" still puzzled at the line of questioning.

"What kind of dog was it?"

"A dingo. Why?" I persisted.

She gave me an odd negative look, shaking her head. That clearly was not the answer she was hoping for.

"Never mind…," she said. She paused, then looked me square in the eyes and said, "Tom, I am talking to your ex-wife!"

I was floored. She did not miss a beat, however, because before I could even respond or digest this news, she began talking rapidly, asking questions, answering them, acting like an interpreter with an invisible foreigner in the room. She would turn to me, and then turn to a vacant spot in the room, as if Alicia were really standing there.

Admittedly much of the "interpreting" was over things that anyone with a creative or deductive mind could declare on behalf of an imaginary spirit if he or she were that cruel.

For example, Alicia said she forgave me (I felt that she did), she gave vague assurances about the afterlife, expressed concern for me and some difficulties I was suffering at the time, and added a few things that any fraudulent clairvoyant would have been sure to add.

But that was not all. Out of the blue, Alicia said, "Remember that time you thought I was trying to talk to you? Well, I was!" She then added if I ever wanted to talk to her again, she would always be there. To enhance my ability to hear her, though, I should try to call to her when I was relaxed and in a quiet place, as if I were meditating. After maybe twenty minutes or half hour, it was over. I could think of no more questions and had nothing more to say.

I was exhausted. I stood up, having this deep sense that Alicia liked Corindee, approved of why she was there, and was almost relieved that someone came along in my life that she could use as an intermediary to get through to me. I hugged Corindee and then left my office, crying quietly, and went to my bedroom where I slept deeply for several hours.

I awoke refreshed. Amazingly, for the first time since her death, I did not feel pain when thinking of Alicia. Rather, I felt closure. I had said good-bye. When I got up and went to my office, I saw that Corindee had gone, leaving a note that she went to see friends. I replayed the entire conversation in my head several times, trying to make sense of it, trying to wrestle with whether or not it had really happened. As I was doing so, it occurred to me how the whole thing started—with the dog.

Whether one believes in spirits, whether one believes in dogs having spirits, I remembered one thing: that dingo, Lucy, was still alive. If Alicia were going to visit me with a dog in tow, it would not be that dog. Indeed, before I had even met her, she had told me about this huge Saint Bernard or similar huge hairy beast she owned—I am not sure what breed, or more accurately, mix of breeds that it belonged to—that she had named Bear. Bear was her first dog, and that one meant a little more. Dog lovers understand. I called up Corindee on her cell phone and asked her, "That dog you saw with Alicia, it wasn't a dingo, was it?"

"No, it wasn't."

"What was it then?"

"A big brown thing. It looked as much like a bear as anything. I figured that when you said dingo that I just got it wrong."

I told her the significance of the dog Bear. She didn't seem too surprised.

Even more time would pass before I would truly appreciate the full significance of that day. I started talking about Alicia and that part of my life to people, people that did not know her as well as those who did. I felt good about the good times, forgave myself for the bad. I was healed.

What is even better, in my own stumbling way, I can communicate with Alicia now. I still don't necessarily hear her talking to me when I call her, but I feel her, I know she is there. If I ask a question, which I don't often do, I don't hear an answer, but I feel one.

Corindee, whose own life was getting much more on track, dropped in one day to say, "I have been thinking a lot about Alicia lately. She's talking to me I think. Is there anything you want to ask her or say to her?"

"No, I'm good," I replied. I figured I could ask her myself.

Thomas Humphrey lives in Boise, Idaho, where he practiced law for many years until 2001 when he took a sabbatical to pursue other interests, including, if he is so fortunate, a writing career. He is currently working on his first novel, a murder mystery set in Sun Valley in the 1930s.

The Visit

by Steven A. Hoffman

"It's going to be a long night," I told my friend John from my cell phone. "I've got another couple hours worth of putting these packets together and I still have to prepare for my speech for tomorrow's meeting."

While assembling the freshly printed materials I had just picked up from Kinko's, a thick-stock cover page for my presentation glided across the palm of my hand like a razor blade slicing through a tomato. I looked at the three-inch cut line. "Uh-oh," I told John, "I just gave myself a massive paper cut. Call me later."

Dropping the phone on the couch, I inspected my wound. First spreading my flesh apart, I separated the cut wider across my hand. Next, I pushed the skin back together. A tiny amount of blood started to bead from the wound, like morning dew on a cobweb. Setting my project aside temporarily, I rushed to the bathroom to doctor my hand.

While at the sink, I heard a noise—like a faint laugh—come from the other room. No one else was in the apartment. I took a look into the mirror and forced myself to change my expression of noticeable fear to one of confidence. I walked cautiously through the dark hallway corner and peeked into my bedroom. My friend Tony was standing beside my bed. We stood about four feet apart, staring at each other.

Frozen stiff from fear and bewilderment, I tried to think… to move… to speak… to scream. Unable to accomplish any of these tasks, I felt a tightness in my entire body, shooting from my jaw to my toes.

Silently examining each other, the air between us seemed thick and dense, cloud-like in mass but completely translucent. It filled the room. Hour-like minutes passed until I finally forced myself to break the stare and the silence.

"Tony? What are you doing here?" The words were soft and slow. My fingers fidgeted uncontrollably as I spoke.

Like he was snapping out of a hypnotic trance, Tony shot awake as his face lit up and a huge friendly grin appeared from ear to ear. I almost broke into a smile too, but the strangeness of the situation prevented any muscles in my mouth from moving.

"Hi, Steve. How are you?" Although Tony did not move, I thought I could actually see energy racing through my friend's body. Tony looked good, even better than the last time we had seen each other, eight months earlier. I looked down at his hands—something was very wrong.

"Uh, I'm fine." I took a hard swallow, feeling a large lump of fear and confusion pass through my mouth, down into the pit of my stomach. "How are you?" I noticed my fingers twitching again.

"I couldn't feel better." He continued to smile, not moving an inch. His eyes were still glued to mine. His speech was articulate.

A quick rush shot to my head, causing me to feel dizzy for a second, and I flashed back to that first day I saw Tony's face on national news. After a few moments, I spoke again.

"Uh, Tony? Do you know…? How d…." There had been many months of concern and sadness that I had felt for my friend, yet I couldn't directly ask that all-important question—the question that had been eating at me night after night for months. Now, finally, I had the chance to get peace of mind. "You're sure you're fine?" My fingers twitched again.

Still smiling, Tony replied, "Yes, of course. Why?"

"You're dea…. You d…. How…?" I watched as Tony's smile faded, showing puzzlement and confusion. Drawing a quick breath, I swallowed another heavy lump. Something else wasn't right. Studying my friend closely, I realized that Tony hadn't moved at all—not even his hands. Yet we were conversing. I clasped my hands together and again the mental image of his gruesome homicide filled my head.

"Tony, do you know what happened?" I asked him anxiously.

"What do you mean? What happened?" Tony's confused questions and still motionless stance lessened my sense of confidence. Tony was here, now, unaware of what had happened to him. It dawned on me that this wasn't a bad thing for Tony not to know.

"Uh, nothing… I just… It's ju… You…." With a quick unsettled smile, I changed approaches. "Never mind. You're fine," I finally said, reassuringly.

"Of course I am!" Tony's grin reappeared. "I've never felt better. I'm very happy. And I'm really happy to see you."

I looked back into Tony's sincere eyes. "And I'm happy to see you, too. I'm glad everything is all right."

From the living room, my cell phone began to ring, breaking the spell of the moment. "That's probably John calling me back," I half-said to myself and to Tony.

Tony smiled widely. "John? How's he doing? I was thinking of visiting him, too. I haven't seen him in ages."

"Well, let me run and get the phone and you can talk with him. He would love to hear from you. Don't go away!" I held up my hands, my palms facing Tony, gesturing for him to stay put.

Answering the phone, I became excited when I heard John's voice. I ran down the hallway to my bedroom, while I yelled into the phone, "Hold it, John, you've got to talk to someone—an old friend. You're going to freak out. You're—"

Tony was no longer in the bedroom. "Aw, man, he's gone. Let me check the other rooms." I ran through each room of my apartment and discovered that it was empty again.

My mind surged as I tried to assess what had just happened. "John, Tony was just here. We were talking to each other."

There was a brief silence from the other end of the phone before John said anything. "Tony? Our friend Tony? Are you OK?"

"Yeah, I'm OK, but this is pretty messed up. I'm serious, John. I was just talking with Tony."

"But Tony's... dead."

"I know! But he was just here—in my bedroom! We were... talking... to each other."

"You and Tony were talking? But...."

I interrupted John. "Yeah, exactly. Tony didn't have his hearing aid. But we were talking. No sign language. He spoke to me—not just the sounds he used to make—but actual words. And he was smiling. He doesn't know what happened." I felt my eyes fill with tears. "He doesn't know. And he said that he's happy."

Having lived in seventeen states and countries, Steve Hoffman has been very happy to call Sioux Falls, South Dakota, home since 1997. When he's not writing, he oversees a seven-gallery visual arts center, a science center with three floors of hands-on exhibits, an Omnimax-type large format theater, and a performing arts center with 1,900- and 300-seat theaters. Steve holds degrees from the University of Illinois and University of Wisconsin and has worked in Chicago, New York, Ann Arbor, Michigan, and Madison, Wisconsin. He is actively involved with a variety of local and national boards, associations, and panels and has been published in several trade publications. He's recently picked up fishing and his one-year-old wirehaired pointing griffon, Gracie, is hoping he'll try his hand at hunting. Steve thanks John, Thea, the Rebels Without a Clause writing group, his family, and friends, and especially Jason for their support. *The Visit* is in memory of Tony.

The Pinecone from Beyond

by Kira Connally

My great-grandparents were farmers in southeastern Nebraska for most of their lives. Archie and Clara Anderson settled on a farm in Odell, Nebraska, in 1949, where they raised crops and cattle. Clara had graduated from Nebraska Wesleyan University in 1930 before she married, a rare thing for a woman then. After her children were raised, she taught math and science at the local school and eventually became principal.

My great-grandfather Archie died in March 1983. I met him when I was three years old, evidenced by photographs, but I don't remember him. I only know him from stories my grandmother Jolene told me and the photographs I've seen. I do remember his grave and his rock collection, always poised on the porch rail, shrinking year by year as we all took a piece home with us. My mother, Wendy, remembered him better, and often she dreamt she was having conversations with him. He had a nickname for her, Sammie, from a book he read when she was a child, and once in a while she would hear that name called out late at night when no one was around.

As a child, I saw Clara on family visits, but I got to know her after I finished high school in 1995. We got to spend time over coffee on snowy winter mornings; mostly she told me stories of life when she was my age in the early 1900s. I found it

36

fascinating, and the more I knew her, the more respect I had for the life she'd lived and the person she had become. The changes in how life is lived from her childhood, where indoor plumbing was a rarity, to our life of cell phones and the Internet are pretty profound.

What interested me most, though, were the stories she would tell about feeling Archie around once in a while, smelling his tobacco, just knowing he was there. By this time it was 1998; he had been dead for fifteen years!

Archie is buried in the corner of a cemetery in Steele City, Nebraska, under a canopy of pine trees. Every time we visited his grave, we'd take home some of the fallen pinecones, where they would sit in bowls with potpourri or find their way onto the Christmas tree. Those pinecones served as a springboard for memories at family gatherings, and they became symbolic of him in my mind.

One of Archie and Clara's interests after they retired was genealogy. Archie himself was one of twelve children (he had over forty cousins!), and family was always very important to both of them. They spent tireless hours writing letters, visiting courthouses, rubbing tombstones. They had quite a lot of information compiled, going back as far as the 1600s in Ireland.

By 2000, I'd become the family genealogist, and whenever I was stumped, I'd pull out one of those pinecones. Soon after, I always found what I was looking for or the name of the person to contact for the information I needed. I fancied they were a connection between Archie's world and mine, a way for me to let him know I was thinking about family, those here and in the hereafter.

I was determined to make use of all that research rather than let it sit in a dusty box in someone's attic, lost to future generations. In seeing photographs and reading old letters and manuscripts about Archie and Clara's life, I finally felt I was getting to know him. Seeing him astride a horse surrounded by cattle on land I'd walked countless times started to give me a sense of him, even though we were far removed by time.

The posed family photos taken years ago in front of rose bushes still blooming in front of the farmhouse made me feel as though I belonged to his family, not just the memories of his family.

By that time I was living in Mineral Wells, Texas, and if you've ever been there, you'll know there is not a pine tree to be found. The piney woods of Texas are about two hundred miles to the east. Cedar, mesquite, and live oaks dotted the area, but nothing so fragile and thirsty as pine. The harsh wind and brutal summer sun would have thwarted any efforts to make one grow.

In the winter of 2001, we knew that Grandma Clara wasn't going to be with us very much longer. Texas is a long way from Nebraska, and I'd only been up to visit once in 2001. Grandma Clara went into the hospital with pneumonia in March 2002, the same month that her husband had died. I started making plans with Grandma Jolene to come up and help her with the funeral and all the things that need to be done when someone passes into the next world. She and I were on the phone late into the night on March 22, and I was still awake the morning of the 23rd when the paper was delivered. I went out onto the front stoop to retrieve it, and in my sleepy state, I picked up the pinecone next to it without even thinking. I put the paper and the pinecone on a table and went to bed.

The coming day was a busy one, and so I never got back to the paper. It wasn't until that night when I learned that Grandma Clara had passed on that I saw the pinecone again. All of a sudden, it was as if all the breath had been sucked out of me. How on earth did a pinecone—an Archie pinecone to me—get on my front stoop?

Though I knew there were no pine trees around, I went outside and looked anyway. None had miraculously appeared anywhere in my yard or the neighbor's yard. When I came back in, I sat with that pinecone, in awe of the message I had been given from my great-grandfather Archie from beyond. Had he been warning me of his wife's coming transition, or merely letting me know he was watching? Whatever the reason, it was proof to me that life goes on after we leave this earth, a comforting thought at a time when a loved one has just died. I took it with me to Nebraska, and after the funeral, I returned it to the gravesite that Archie and Clara now shared.

Growing up in a spooky family, Kira Connally couldn't help but develop an interest in the paranormal and the unexplained. She grew up on her grandmother's stories of the mediums in Lily Dale, New York, her mother's tarot cards, astrology books, and the whispers that no matter where in the country her family moved, spirits seemed to follow them. She learned to read cards at a young age, and has avid interests in mythology, psychology, and the paranormal. Kira has a background in team training and optics, and works as an optician in Weatherford, Texas. She is also a tour guide at the haunted Baker Hotel in Mineral Wells, Texas. She ghost hunts with Mystic Ghost (http://www.mysticghost.com) based in Fort Worth, Texas, a team that combines science with psychic ability to validate the presence of ghosts and spirits. Kira is currently enrolled in the Morris Pratt Institute. She can be contacted through her web site http://www.blueivvy.com.

Four Legs and the Bridge Home

by Ellen Lane

"Just go, already," I grumbled at Mom. "Go. Please? Quit worrying about things here."

"Well…," she hedged. "I'm not sure I should leave right now."

"Just go," I repeated for the fourth time.

"But…."

"Mom," I said as I gently began herding her out the door, "I promise to visit Granny every day."

I spent fifteen more frustrating minutes getting Mom in the car and on her way. Promised more promises, and got lots more instructions from her.

Finally, she left. I was exhausted.

Getting Mom to go anywhere these days was like rolling a rock uphill.

You see my grandmother was in a nursing home.

Grandma had moved in with Mom and me some thirty years ago. Right after my dad beat a hasty exit. And except for one brief gap when she remarried, Grandma had lived exclusively with my mother ever since.

But at the age of ninety, she suffered a massive stroke.

It was Granny's last physical fumble in her ten-year scrimmage with heart attacks, pacemakers, radical mastectomies, broken backs, and cataracts.

Consigned to a nursing home for the rest of her life. Benched. Game over.

My mother became her full-time care overseer for six, long years.

Mom paid her daily visits. Then, in between the mountains of Granny's laundry, she hassled with Medicare, Medicaid, and the nursing facility, and brought Grandma home on a regular basis.

But as the years pressed on, those visits home became every other weekend. Then once a month. Then only on holidays.

The loading, unloading, and even the short trek into the house became too taxing for anyone who helped. Nerves, muscles, and backs got strained to the maximum.

At home, Grandma could not be left alone for one minute. Mom literally could not go to the bathroom without fearing that Grandma would try to stand, or worse. She thought her body was doing exactly what she told it to. Nothing we could do or say could convince Grandma that her own legs were no longer trustworthy.

From her wheelchair, Grandma would argue soundly that she was standing, thank you very much. It was part comedy. Mostly tragedy.

Toilet breaks assumed nightmarish qualities. Grandma was far too heavy for any less than two of us to handle. Even then, we often found ourselves grappling with one hundred and fifty pounds of limp flesh, sometimes trying to scrape her off the floor or lift her from a noodley heap.

So that afternoon, I was glad that Mom had gone on a well-deserved vacation, that she was leaving the responsibility of Grandma to me. For a week or so, anyway.

On my way to the nursing home, I popped into Safeway and bought some strawberries, one of Granny's favorite fruits. I carried my treasure into Grandma's room.

"Hi there," I said with impressive cheerfulness. "How are you feeling today?"

Her head lolled toward me from the pillow. Slowly she recognized me. Well, almost. She coughed. Sputtered out, "Jean… where's Jessie?"

Jean is my mother. Jessie is mother's twin sister.

"This is Ellen, honey. Remember?"

More coughing. "Oh, yeah, that's right." Phlegm crowded the barely recognizable words up her throat. Her breathing rattled like a baby's toy.

Hoo-boy, I thought. This is bad.

"I brought you some strawberries. Would you like to try some?"

Eating was horrible for her. The last mini stroke had affected her tongue and throat. She had trouble knowing if the food was in her mouth or when it was going down. Her swallowing mechanism didn't cooperate any more that her legs did. My mind wandered as I dabbed tastes of mashed berries on her tongue.

How many times had she claimed the lady in the next bed was having children sleep over? What number of kittens and puppies were we up to that she'd rescued since being here? And just how much money had she won (again) in the lottery?

I knew how hard this was on me, but what must it be like for her? A small, sad smile traced my lips.

I washed her chin and cleaned her hands. Then gently applied lotion over her face. It was a tiny pleasure to watch her expression smooth out. See a ghost of her old grin (mostly a one-sided grimace now) brighten the room. She mumbled terribly. In the last months her speech had all but disintegrated. I had to say "What?" over and over again.

But tonight, after a few of those "Whats?" she got exasperated.

"I'm nod dunna talg no mo. All you shay id WHUH!" she spat out at last. Her most articulate speech in a while and her meaning crystal clear.

"You're right," I said, crisscrossing my fingers over my heart. "I'm sorry. I won't say 'what' anymore."

Under all the frozen muscles, Granny was still in there. Spiky and ornery.

She inclined her head in agreement, almost regally. Then relaxed against the pillow.

I combed her wispy, white hair away from her forehead with my fingers and whispered "goodnight sweetie." Smooched her brow and went to track down the night-duty nurse. Find out what they were doing for her latest case of pneumonia.

That night I dreamt.

The lush landscape gently rolled away from me. Green and fertile as far as the eye could see. Lazy, forever knolls of trimmed grass that rivaled any golf course.

Trees stood out in vivid relief. Gathered here and there in small oases. Their mixed hues of evergreen, forest, and emerald a perfect contrast against the backdrop of dazzling blue. In the sky, dainty puffs of pure white floated magically by. Cotton balls and fuzzy bunnies suspended in the atmosphere. Such peace. Such serenity. How to describe the overwhelming tranquility? Impossible.

My busy brain stilled. My heart slowed. Fresh air filled me like a helium balloon. Giddiness blossomed. Drunkenly, I bent to brush the thick velvet grass under my bare feet. I pressed my hand down. A fresh mowed scent lingered in the air.

This place, this space was absolute perfection. Vast and limitless.

I flung my arms wide. An ant in front of a mountain.

Motion on the far horizon drew my attention. Many tiny shapes had crested a small rise. I squinted my eyes and the shimmering forms coalesced into animals.

Dozens of them. All heading straight for me.

Yet I felt no shudder of panic. I was simply not afraid.

If my heart were the shore, they came as the tide. Wave after wave, in love.

Recognition surged through me as they neared. These were my beloved pets of long ago. All of them gone now.

There was Perry, my first dog. Bootsie, my first cat. My Bouvier Napoleon and Peppy the Chihuahua. Smokie and Sam. Snooks and Sandy. Hildy and Ted. Dogs and cats. Rabbits and rescued birds.

Approaching me with carefree abandon, their faces lit with joy.

Crowding in around me with affection and love like I haven't felt in ages. Bestowing the greatest of gifts—remembrance.

I hunkered down to meet them. Wet and rough tongues alike found my chin. Fur danced between my fingers. Tails snapped and snaked around my back. Whiskers delightedly tickled my knees. Together we petted and cooed. It felt good. Like coming home.

Their loose huddle began to waver slowly. Undulating me along in their midst.

They were herding and coaching me across the hills. Leading me over the sweet, green grass.

Come along. Come along, they said. Come with us. Look around. See. All this is beauty and happiness. Isn't this a wonderful place?

I went easily with my friends. Carried by weightless feet we toured the rolling hills and shadowed valleys. Enjoyed playful cascading streams and majestic woodlands. Marveled at flowering meadows and fat grazing horses.

They continued to urge me on and on, faster, until we were fairly flying across the land.

Again and again telling me the wonder and beauty of where they lived.

We will be here to greet her, they all thought-spoke together. Look where she will be. Sharing this splendor with us. We will take care of her. She will like it here. There will be no more pain.

At that, I cried.

The tears woke me. My pillow was wet, my lips stretched in an idiotic and radiant smile.

I had been visited by all of my deceased pets. Each one a dear departed friend.

Reaching into my dream space, they had allowed me to see the serenity of their world. Assure me of their happiness. And that they still loved me.

Letting me know that they would be there to greet Grandma as she came over.

Understanding seeped in like syrup over pancakes. Heavy. Numbing and sweet at the same time.

The phone shrilled into the silence of the bedroom.

I rose and padded across the room, already knowing what the voice on the other end would say. Already fumbling through my address book for Mom's hotel number.

After ninety-six years, Grandma had died.

But she had friends on the other side. They told me so. And I believe them.

Ellen Lane is a native of the beautiful Pacific Northwest. She began writing small scenes from her life, but quickly acknowledged that writing was a way to stay alive. Ellen is a wife, mother, grandmother, Wiccan, professional belly dancer, published poet, and author.

Daddy's Favorite Song

by Sandy Williams Driver

My daddy loved country music. He used to tell me stories about his family gathering around their old Zenith radio back in the early 1930s and listening to the latest bluegrass tunes each Saturday night on the live Grand Ole Opry broadcast.

The late 1940s brought the haunting voice over the airways of the man my daddy always proclaimed to be "the best country music singer of all time"—Hank Williams. As far as I know, the legendary performer was no relation to my father, Dalton Williams, even though both men were tall and thin with beautiful eyes.

As a child, I often sat beside Daddy as he listened with a hint of a smile to one of the many Hank Williams' 45 records he owned. I remember watching the small black circle spin on the turntable and listening respectfully to the enduring voice tinged with a slow, Southern drawl and a touch of static.

Over the years, Daddy replaced his LPs with eight-track tapes and then a little later with small cassette tapes. He always bought every Hank Williams selection he could find.

In the mid-1990s, my sister bought a CD player for Dad. He liked it immensely and of course, the first CD he bought was *20 of Hank Williams' Greatest Hits.*

He thought it was grand that he could push a button and immediately hear a specific song anywhere on the disk. Daddy loved all the songs recorded by Hank Williams, including "Your Cheatin' Heart" and "Kaw-Liga," but his favorite tune was "Hey, Good Lookin'," which was number 13 on the CD. He would sit and listen to it over and over again.

A few weeks after my daddy died of cancer on May 28, 1999, my mother brought a trunk full of boxes over to my house. She had kept a few of Dad's personal belongings, but had decided to give me some of my father's memorabilia.

We sat down in the floor of my den and began sifting through the memories of his life. In the bottom of a large box, underneath a stack of neatly pressed handkerchiefs, I found an old, faded and yellowed newspaper article dated 1953. It was clipped from a tabloid in Montgomery, Alabama, and told the distressing news of the death of the beloved country music singer Hank Williams at the young age of twenty-nine.

Mother had no idea where Daddy had gotten the newspaper or why he had kept it. But because he thought it was important enough to keep, I folded it carefully and placed it in my scrapbook for future generations to read.

In another box, I found the Hank Williams greatest hits CD my dad had listened to so many times. I smiled and asked Mom why she didn't want to keep it for herself. "That CD player stopped working a few months before your daddy died and I haven't gotten around to buying another one," she told me.

I had no idea it was broken and thought it was sad that Daddy didn't get to listen to his favorite CD during the weeks before his death.

After Mom left, I put everything back in the boxes and left them in the den.

It was getting late and my breaking heart just couldn't hold up to opening another container of reminders of Daddy that day.

I went to bed around 10 p.m. and fell into a deep sleep. At exactly midnight, my husband and I were abruptly awakened by the blaring sound of our stereo in the living room. We jumped out of bed and raced down the hall, expecting to see one of our young sons up on a stool messing with the knobs on our sound system, which was on the top shelf of our entertainment center.

The darkness of the living room greeted us and sent us scrambling to find the light switch. The bright glow revealed no playful children, just an empty room.

My husband rushed over to the stereo and reached up to turn the power off when I stopped him.

A chill ran down my spine as I pointed to the open CD case lying on a middle shelf of the entertainment center. I picked it up and gasped aloud when I closed it to reveal the title—*20 of Hank Williams' Greatest Hits*. I stared open-mouthed at my husband as number 13, "Hey, Good Lookin'," played over and over again.

The children had been awakened by the loud music also and stumbled into the living room with sleep-filled eyes. "What's going on?" they asked.

I really had no idea how to answer their question. I knew, as the last person to go to bed that night, that Daddy's CD had been left in a box downstairs in the den. Two hours later, it was in the living room, in the CD player, and set to play a specific song repeatedly.

My husband gave me a warm smile before kneeling in front of the children. "It's just your Paw Paw listening to his favorite song."

Today, three years later, I still have the Hank Williams CD sitting beside my stereo. I carefully take it out of the case and play it in its entirety at least once or twice a month. I always stop on number 13 and play it an extra couple of times—just for Daddy.

Sandy Williams Driver, and husband, Tim, live in Albertville, Alabama, where both were born and raised. They have three children, Josh, Jake, and Katie. Sandy is a full-time writer with numerous publishing credits in her resume. Her articles and essays have won numerous awards and appeared in over fifty magazines, newspapers, and anthologies across the United States, Australia and England. She is a member of the Alabama Writer's Conclave, a column editor for *U.S. Legacies*, a small nostalgia magazine in Indiana, and writes a weekly parenting column for her local newspaper, *The Sand Mountain Reporter*. Her first novel, *The Lights of Home*, will be released in January 2005 from Behler Publications. She loves to hear from readers via SandyDriver@aol.com.

The Ghost of Mr. Kelly

by Thanea A. Martin Kelly

OK, so it sounds like a bad joke. What do you do when you meet the ghost of your father-in-law? In my case, I write a story about it. But, you see, I really loved my father-in-law. Joe Kelly was a fantastic guy. We got along famously. We talked about everything, and I would listen to the same old family stories for the umpteenth time. He would sit by the pool, smoking an occasional cigar. He supported my decision to attend grad school and pushed my husband to finish his undergraduate degree. He was always there for us.

Then, when I was six months pregnant with his first grandchild, Mr. Kelly had a massive heart attack and died. It did not seem possible. A month before, he and Mrs. Kelly had promised to come visit us in Atlanta and buy a crib for the nursery. With his service in the Air Force Reserve and a thirty-year career working for the Defense Department, it seemed most appropriate to bury him at Barrancas National Cemetery at N.A.S. Pensacola with full military honors on Memorial Day. It was moving and heartbreaking. I can still remember singing "Because He Lives" at the funeral.

Life went on for my husband, Warren, and me five hours away. We had a nursery to set up and doctor appointments to attend. We knew life was more difficult for Warren's mother and sister. They were confronted with the trappings of Mr. Kelly's life on a daily basis.

In late June we went back for a visit. Warren and I arrived in ninety-degree heat, ready for a quick dip in the pool. We changed into our swimsuits and went out back. As Mrs. Kelly worked in the kitchen, Warren and I chatted in the pool. Suddenly, I smelled the scent of cigar smoke. I didn't say anything. It had to be my imagination, right?

After that trip, Mrs. Kelly started telling Warren about strange shadows in the house. They would appear suddenly and disappear again. Since she is such a religious woman, she called them angels. I still remembered that cigar smoke. I had never heard of an angel who smoked cigars.

Time came and went. My beautiful daughter, Montgomery, was born in August. My wonderful grandmother died in September. We visited Pensacola once every couple of months, but nothing more happened. I had all but forgotten the incident. Then we celebrated Christmas.

Warren, Montgomery, and I came the week after Christmas. The first day we were in Pensacola we celebrated Christmas, much like we always had. It wasn't quite the same without Mr. Kelly, but that was to be expected. After a couple of days, my daughter started really suffering from the teething pain she had been experiencing for a couple of weeks. She had been screaming for an hour by 10:15 p.m., when my mother-in-law and husband headed out to find medicine to calm her down. While they were gone, I sat in the lounge chair that my father-in-law had always used, rocking and soothing my daughter. After fifteen more minutes of screaming and crying and murmuring, Montgomery calmed down.

The History Channel was showing *Haunted Caribbean* that night and I looked up to watch as I rocked my now-quiet daughter.

As I did, a shadow swept across the room. It walked toward the television, where it paused for a moment. Then it turned and walked up the hallway to my right. When I looked at the clock, it was 10:37. Every night, Mr. Kelly watched the local news at 10:00. Then he would go to bed and watch *The Tonight Show*. I sat there and whispered, "Mr. Kelly?" This time I knew I was not imagining it.

I told Warren that night, because I was so shocked. My husband is a skeptic. So it took a lot of nerve for me to say anything. He said it was a car passing outside, but the shadow moved from left to right, not right to left as it does with headlights in the den. We decided not to say anything to his mother. It was hard enough already.

Three months later, Mrs. Kelly and Sarah were discussing some of the odd things they had seen in the house recently. Mainly, they heard noises or saw shadows, much like I had seen. Before I realized it, I was telling the story of that night. They were not surprised. In fact I think it was a comfort to know someone else had seen them too.

Angels or ghosts? Residual energy or phantom presence? I cannot prove the science behind what I saw. I just know I did. Did Mr. Kelly come to comfort the granddaughter he was never allowed to see in this life? Or was it a faded memory fulfilling itself in front of me? I guess I'll never really know, but I know what I believe. Hamlet was right; there are a lot of things in this life we will never know about.

However, as I sit here again in his chair in the very same room in which I faced my last encounter, my laptop does not seem to want to work quite right. My husband says it's a short in the power cable. But I'm not so sure. Maybe Mr. Kelly wants to us to keep this story to ourselves.

Thanea Kelly is a history teacher at East High School in Sciotoville, Ohio. She is the wife of a seminary student and the mother of a beautiful three-year-old daughter. A graduate of Liberty University, Thanea is an active member of First Baptist Church of Greenup, Kentucky, participating in the music program and working in Sunday School. She also enjoys reading, traveling, and many crafts.

One Lone Penny

by Bill Webb

It should have been me who died from liver damage. I had been the alcoholic, not him. But my brother was too far gone for a transplant. On his last night his wife told him it was OK to leave, that we would be fine and he could just go to sleep. He shook his head frantically as his lips attempted to form the word "no," and with fear in his eyes, he went to sleep for the last time. At first I thought he was afraid for himself, but soon discovered for whom he was really afraid. I ought to have known. Everyone knew what he was like. His work here was not done and he didn't stay away.

Chuck was always a helper beyond the call of duty. They would call from the factory in the middle of the night because a machine he designed was on the fritz, and before dawn he would have fixed the machine and returned in time to snow plow his neighbor's driveway so they could get to work. You could always count on him to fix anything, applying his mechanical prowess without complaint. He was so busy helping others he had neglected his first love, fishing. What a waste, I selfishly thought. He could easily afford a fishing boat and go every weekend if he wanted. People just take advantage of him. My lack of understanding his seemingly misplaced priorities took a one-eighty only after he was gone.

It was a year later that I noticed the pennies appearing at critical moments. Mom and Frank had already noticed but did not get the connection. Mom did not remember that Chuck had a penny collection when we were kids and had collected every year except a couple of Indian Heads and the infamous "1909-S VDB" he always boasted was the most valuable of them all. No one knew what became of the collection.

Frank had come into the picture twenty years after Mom's divorce and had bonded with Chuck right away, drawn by their humanitarian and mechanical inclinations. Frank worked in a pro shop building and repairing golf clubs.

One day, a customer swooped down on Frank with expletives about slow service and incompetence and why did he even trust him in the first place. Speechless, Frank picked up the repair slip and underneath was a lone penny. He looked up at the man and his whole countenance changed as if a hypnotist had said the key word and snapped his fingers. The man was smiling and calm and as happy as could be.

Frank put the penny in his pocket, thinking maybe it was good luck, but never thought of Chuck. More pennies began appearing at key moments seeming to trigger a change in attitude from confusion, anger, or frustration to kindness, gentleness, and generosity.

Then Mom noticed it happening too. On a grumpy, pain-filled morning she opened her locker at work and a penny seemed to jump out at her, practically startling her off her feet. She held it in her hand and suddenly an overwhelming sense of peace came over her and the pain disappeared. But it wasn't until my experience that we got the connection and knew Chuck was doing for us what we could not do for ourselves.

I was on a self-promotion auto trip from Texas to Nashville, Boston, and New York. I was fully armed with copies of my best songs, demo tapes, promo packs, and 8 by 10 black and white glossies of my favorite singer/songwriter—me. I had a few appointments but mostly was improvising and trying to make connections with anyone who was anyone in the music industry I could find. In Nashville, I met with Tim McGraw's people and got nowhere. I investigated possible contacts through BMI, the musician's union, and *Songwriter Magazine* but failed to come up with any concrete leads. I left Nashville certain that my alleged talent was a myth begun by my mother, drove to the Blue Ridge Mountains, and pitched my tent.

That night, I pulled out my laptop to look at my agenda and paused to listen. I could hear the rushing of a powerful stream and imagined the trees trembling furiously as a strong wind shook my tent. Thunder was drawing closer and the skies were threatening to drop a deluge upon my little domed haven. Thinking I was going to write another song, I began to type.

Bill was happy this morning. Though his expression had the blankness learned after years of practice hiding feelings, his eyes did not lie. They never could. They were bright and alive and seemed to light up his whole face. Perhaps it was a subtle upturn at the corners of his mouth, the slight rise in his puffy, baby-like cheeks, or the slight squint in his eyes that made them look like upside-down half-moons. He was happy and Beth was relieved to see it. She had been walking on eggshells long enough and was just about at the end of her rope. One more day of that torturous glare, the cynical responses to even the most innocent of queries, the begrudging way he did any kind of favor complete with tirades on the miseries of his little world including her ineptitudes, and she would burst.

I read and reread those lines. Would I ever be happy? How long had it been since I had even cracked a smile? How miserable was I making everyone around me? Since Chuck left? Maybe all my life, though I spent so much of it trying to fool people into believing I was such an upbeat fellow. Ha! I was a living black cloud spreading darkness everywhere. Just my luck that nothing on this trip was working out. And now I would probably get washed away by the storm. A welcome alternative as far as I could see.

I went to sleep as usual, totally self-absorbed with my miserable life and haunted by fears of impending doom amplified by every crack of thunder.

The gray, wet dawn confronted me with the task of packing a soggy tent and keeping my guitar and laptop from getting wet. After an hourlong struggle, I was ready to leave. One more look at the campsite and there, in the center of the dry patch where the tent had been, was a lone penny. I was not sure why it caught my attention, but I picked it up and read the year of my brother's death. The significance came to me and I knelt and cried uncontrollably. Somehow, he was here trying to get my attention. Out came a flood of childhood memories of big brother lessons about how to water-ski and catch grass snakes and use power tools.

If only he were here now and could tell me how to live life!

I pocketed the penny and drove on toward Boston with no clue where to go or who to see. In D.C. I took a brief detour to the Mall and walked along the Vietnam Veterans Memorial. Chuck served there and I thought his name should be engraved on the wall now that he too was a casualty. I walked up to the W's just to see if there were any Webbs there, and directly below was one lone penny. I picked it up to read once again the year of my brother's death. Patriotism does not bide well with the self-centered, yet at that moment I saw the heroism and courage it took for Chuck to enlist and fight for our country. I began to see the priceless gift of freedom, and a wave of gratitude for being born in America filled me with peace.

In Boston I was totally directionless. I had pitched my tent at a campsite just south of town and was beginning to wonder how I would be able to buy food. The cash was low, I needed gas, and I was sure I had reached the limit on my credit card. I parked at the far end of a grocery store parking lot and sat in silence. Suddenly, a chicken delivery truck barreled into the lot, swerving around me, and a penny came flying up out of nowhere and landed on my hood. I picked it up to read still again the year of my brother's death. With a newfound confidence, I strutted into the store, bought all the groceries I needed with the credit card, and called my mother.

"Chuck's talking to me with pennies!" I burst out. "There's a penny every time I need something and he's there! Talking to me!"

Mom proceeded to tell me about the pennies she and Frank had been finding and I got even more excited. "It's Chuck, using his collection to help us, to make things work out!" She had not remembered the penny collection or gotten the connection, but she was convinced.

Now you could easily claim coincidence and say that, from this point on, finding pennies was just a self-fulfilling prophecy. But how do you explain this: The first story I ever got published was a penny story. And I did not even know I was a writer! I wear a small pierced earring that looks like a penny. A publisher sees it and says, "My, how interesting. Why are you wearing a penny in your ear?" I tell her about my brother and relate one of my dozens of penny stories and she says, "We are publishing a book about real-life encounters with people after they died. Why don't you write one or two of those stories of yours and submit it to me?"

The rest is history, but there is more. From the day in the grocery store parking lot to this day, I have seen life as a blessing filled with opportunities to love and serve. I have seen myself as having valuable abilities I can use to contribute to life in worthwhile ways.

Self-absorption is slowly slipping away and being replaced with character traits I could only attribute to my brother. I know he did not just die and leave a legacy. He continues to guide me in the ways of helpfulness and concern for others. The pennies remind me that I am in the right place at the right time and all will work out.

Just the other day, I went to my twelve-step meeting with no money in my wallet. I always like to put a dollar in the basket at the end of the meeting as a personal show of gratitude. I grabbed my little red coin purse, certain that it must contain at least a dollar. As I spilled it out on the table and began counting nickels, dimes, and pennies, I became concerned I would not have enough. I counted the last pennies, 98 cents, 99 cents, one dollar. And left in my little red coin purse was one lone penny!

Bill Webb is a composer, arranger, musician, and entertainer. With his first published short story, he is also well on his way as a serious writer of prose. Currently editing his first novel, Bill also has several short stories in the works. "Writing has always been my first love; I just never had the courage to pursue it as a career until now," says Bill. Bill's affinity for the written word began at age five when his teachers discovered he could spell and read the words from the fifth-grade spelling list. He credits his high school English composition teacher, best-selling author Peter Straub (*Ghost Story*, *The Talisman* with Stephen King, and seventeen other novels), with the inspiration and tools to pursue creative writing.

After several years of playing keyboard and touring with musical acts across the United States, including Corey and Company, The Lloyd Pedersen Show, and Bill Webb Live, Bill has settled down in Bedford, Texas, with his wife, Beth, and their cat, Hearty.

As vice president of B & B Yoga and Music LLC, Bill operates a music studio that produces CDs of original compositions. He also teaches piano, guitar, voice, and drums and coaches children and adults in the performing arts. He enjoys a daily personal yoga practice, which keeps him forever young and healthy. Visit him at www.billwebb.biz.

The Light of Good-bye

by Wendy Kay Strain

I t was about 2 in the morning when I woke up from a frightening dream.

In the dream, I was alone. My family had left me and I was living in a stranger's house trying to act like a grown-up, but realizing I was still an innocent kid. In the dream, the world was black and gray. I was hungry, but there was no money to buy food. I was cold, but I didn't have a home to return to. I was alone because no one could join me. The entire dream was suffused with a feeling of overwhelming panic. It was with a stifled scream that I bolted awake.

I woke to the room of a stranger.

It took me a moment or two to remember I was in the home of some family friends, in their guest room to be exact. They had agreed to take me in when my parents and siblings followed their next adventure up north four months before I graduated from high school. It was coldly impersonal, neither masculine nor feminine. It had been two months, but I still hadn't accustomed myself to waking up in this blank space of a room.

The room was dark, but I could see the red glowing lines of the clock radio. After the emotions of the dream, the light looked evil, angry, menacing. I was still frightened from the dream.

I moved a pillow over the light to keep it from seeing me as I focused on the dark outlines of the dresser across the room. The table lamp perched on the dresser top had a white shade that carried a slight glow from the streetlight three houses down. The mirror on the wall next to it cast eerie shadows across the foot of my bed.

Taking shaky breaths, I tried to calm myself by focusing on the dim light. As I watched, it seemed to grow, expanding misty rays outward and upward but not growing any brighter.

With surprise, I suddenly realized I was looking up at the figure of a human being, an adolescent boy, younger than I but not by a lot.

As the light continued to pour from the frame, I started to recognize the facial features of the boy. His slight shoulders were carried straighter than when I had last seen him. An aura of suffering that had once enveloped him was no longer visible, but the form was unmistakably that of my younger brother.

In our ever-changing family, he was actually my stepbrother, but the two of us were closer than blood relations. He was the only person I knew who could understand the wide-roving nature of my imagination, and I was the only person he knew that could follow his lengthy scientific ideas. In our world, we were each other's best and only real friend.

This wasn't the first time I had woken in the night to see him standing at the foot of my bed. Sometimes we would even manage to say a word or two to each other in the time since he had moved away.

I knew he had been very sick. Even if my mother hadn't called me to let me know, I could see it in these occasional apparitions, his frame growing thinner, his shoulders braced under the weight of a tremendous pain, the pinched look in his eyes and the desperate light that fluttered within.

But he had never appeared like this. Always before when I had seen him, he had appeared as a hologram image might, full of color, wearing his normal clothes, but somewhat transparent.

Now he was full of light, so full that I couldn't make out what clothes he was wearing. There was no color, only the light. Maybe it was that idea alone that frightened me so much. He shouldn't be so bright.

He didn't say anything, but as we sat looking at each other, the terror in the room slowly faded to a growing realization of what we were facing.

I started to cry. I couldn't help it. There was so much loss in the room I couldn't bear it. I had lost my best friend; he had lost a lifetime of dreams come true. The thought occurred to me that I had never told him how much he had always meant to me.

He reached his arm out to me, but I couldn't feel anything more than a cool, almost imperceptible breeze. The cool feeling of that breeze traveled up my arm and dried my tears, softening the burning lump that had formed in my throat.

Yes, there was loss, but there couldn't have been a win. His disease had no cure, he had already suffered years of invasive medical treatments, and his body was too weak to hold on.

But there was also gain. I understood with that touch that he was now free. The pain no longer held him captive. For that, we should rejoice. He could now explore those places that we always planned on going together. He could go farther than that even. He had finally managed to find a way to explore a place our parents hadn't been before was the wry joke that stopped in the air between us.

Caught in the middle, we could neither laugh nor cry. We could only stare.

What about Mom and Dad? What about our other brother, the one that worried constantly about getting sick himself?

It was not going to be easy, we decided. What would they do? What was I going to do?

The tears threatened again. Who would keep my feet on the ground now that the only one who understood the paths I usually walked would be gone?

With a tilt of his head he wondered what made me think we would ever be apart. As long as there was love, there would be a way for us to connect.

Then he started to fade. He left in the same way he had come, slowly dissipating back into the mist and then the faint streetlight softly falling across the foot of my bed. I stared at that light until the rising sun chased it away.

When I had gone to sleep that night, the only facts I knew about my brother's health was that his cancer had come out of remission. He had already overcome the illness three times by the time he was fourteen, so there was no real reason to be overly concerned. He had been undergoing new treatment for two weeks already and seemed to be responding well.

I floated through the next day, wrapped in my own protective fog. I dreaded the sound of anyone's voice, afraid they would come tell me the news that my brother had died. It was inconceivable. He was fine the last time I talked with my family, and that had been only four days ago.

It came when I least expected it. I had returned to the house for a quick snack before a school function when the woman I was living with called me into the kitchen. Her eyes were red and she was holding the phone in her hand.

"Your mother wants to talk with you," she said, relinquishing the phone into my lifeless hands.

"I know." I spoke into the phone with a dead voice that was not my own. "All I want to know is why."

The explanation was lengthy, full of tears and medical jargon, but it boiled down to a case of the flu that quickly escalated into pneumonia with his depleted immune system and the doctors couldn't get it under control fast enough. They did everything they could do.

Time of death: 1:57 a.m.

———————

Wendy Strain spends most of her time working as a full-time news editor for a small local newspaper near her home in Dallas, Texas, where she lives with her husband and teenage daughter. The house also plays host to two cats, Oliver and Simba, who have apparently decided to stay.

In her "spare" time, she enjoys working on freelance writing, editing, and graphic design projects; creative writing; artistic endeavors; and spending time with her family. Samples of her work, both professional and creative, along with the various services she currently offers, are highlighted on her web site at www.writeservices.net.

Although her working experience deals with "just the facts," Wendy was trained in creative writing for children and majored in English at Texas Wesleyan University. She's currently finishing a second bachelor's degree in graphic design at Westwood College, utilizing the best that the Internet has to offer through online education.

Out of the studio, Wendy enjoys swimming, walking, roller blading, staying in shape, and exploring whatever life has to offer. She remains close to her extended family, having two brothers, a nephew, and parents living nearby, and shares an interest in the family business—child care—through her work on the company's marketing endeavors.

Five White Horses

by Dana Buchanan

I remember my grandmother saying whenever she dreamed of five white horses someone was going to die. She never harmed crickets in the house, saying it was bad luck, and would always capture them gently and let them go outside. She would put a pot full of water under my aunt's bed during a full moon. I grew up with her doing things like this and they always intrigued me. She mixed these so-called superstitions with a strong belief in God and always made me feel blessed and protected.

Growing up I was always a bit curious, even a little jealous, of these gifts my grandmother had; I wanted to have dreams and intuitions so I could feel what she felt. I wanted to see the future and help people. But as a child I did not say much. No one did actually; few even acknowledged it. It was just how our lives were. I am sure outsiders would have thought the pans of water under the bed were strange, but they were routine to us.

As I grew older I saw this was not so much a blessing but more of some sort of curse, especially for my grandmother. She would have nightmares, or so we called them for lack of a better word, when in fact they were more like visions while she was awake. This is one thing that was passed on to my mother. I can remember her having horrible nightmares and waking up crying and screaming. And again no one ever talked about this. Little did I realize that I indeed had inherited some of these so-called gifts.

I was in my late teens and my mother's best friend passed away. My mother and Chris had been friends since their teens. She had always been involved in my life. I admired and looked up to her. She was a free spirit who fit perfectly into any situation from a business office to a wild party, having friends in every walk of life. When she passed away not only did I grieve for my mother and the loss of her best friend, but I too felt the loss. Without her around there was an emptiness that could not be ignored. There were so many things that I wanted to talk to her about, get her advice on, etc. I felt like we had been cheated, that even though we knew she was dying there was not enough time to fit the rest of my life in and get her advice on what could happen in my future. I know that sounds selfish, but I wanted her to live forever.

A few weeks after she passed away, I had really been thinking of her and wishing I could help my mother with the loss. I fell asleep but felt awake; it was a sort of pre-slumber state. That's when I had this amazing feeling. It was a calm feeling. I opened my eyes and felt as if I were watching a dream.

I have never had an out-of-body experience, but can imagine this is what it would feel like. I saw myself sitting on a couch, the couch Chris had. As I looked around I noticed I was in her apartment. Then I felt myself sitting on the couch—not watching anymore but actually sitting on the couch. I felt that I was really there. I blinked a few times to see if I could wake up, but could not. I was in another place, maybe another time. I could smell her perfume and nail polish lingering in the air. It made me confused but calm.

Then the door opened and I saw Chris and my mom walk in with arms full of shopping bags. Shopping was a guilty pleasure that made them happy, when they could find the time and money to do so. I was startled and stood up, backing my way against the wall and feeling the wall's texture on my hands and the coldness of the wood floor on my feet. I could not believe it was her standing there in front of me. Was this what a ghost looked like? I started to cry, I had missed her so much. She smiled and touched my cheek and told me everything was OK. I remember mumbling, "No, you're dead." That was all I could blurt out. She smiled again and told me she was gone but would always be with me. She laughed and looked so happy. She told me she wanted to talk to Mom again and she missed her a lot.

Then everything disappeared and it was just the two of us. We were just standing together in emptiness. It was as if the illusion of her and my mother was just to calm me, to show me that Chris was happy and OK. She looked at me and said she was OK and wanted me to tell my mom she was OK and would always be watching over me. She smiled her priceless smile and assured me things would be fine and I should not ever be scared of things like this.

She also explained why she did not appear to my mother. She felt Mom was so upset and not in the right frame of mind to allow her to come back in yet and to bring her to this place. This statement confused me at first. But I think Mom's mind was too distraught to allow Chris in at the moment. As she disappeared, I blinked, closing my eyes tight at first then opening them; I was in my bed.

I truly believe she visited me that night. I told my mom about the dream the next day and relayed the message Chris had given me. My mother smiled and for the first time since Chris's death she had tears of joy. She said she felt better and felt like Chris was really there with us, and that she was OK now.

A few years passed, and I had not had any other visions or felt any other feelings. I thought maybe I had dreamed it all and was having my doubts about these inherited gifts. Then I started having these dreams about little things.

I dreamed that the office were I worked was robbed. And the next morning when I went into work a coworker told me that someone had broken in and took the TV and VCR from the conference room.

This made no sense to me. What good did these dreams do? They were silly and did not even seem to be predictions; they seemed to happen while the event I dreamed of was happening.

When my grandmother passed away I waited and waited for her to visit me in my dreams. I don't recall her ever doing that. Then several years after she passed away I had another "pre-slumber" dream but this time it was mixed with a bit of a real event. This vision was short. My grandmother had called me on my cell phone and said she was ready to be picked up from the hospital, that she had been there long enough.

I was shocked to hear her voice and kept asking her how she got my number, thinking it was a joke. I said I would be right down, and sure enough as I pulled up to the hospital, there was my grandmother sitting on the curb and waiting for me. But she almost did not recognize me. She kept asking, "Now which one are you? Whose daughter are you?" I felt as if this was my grandmother but in a different time maybe.

She asked me a few questions and wanted to talk to my mom. She wanted to go to her old house and have everyone get together. Then she requested that I call everyone and have them meet us. She wanted to see our children and her other two grandchildren. She took my hand, squeezing it gently to assure me that this was all OK. Then the dream ended.

I had no real message to give anyone. I did not even have the so-called out-of-body experience or understand the dream entirely. But right as I woke up I had a frantic phone call from my mom. She said that something strange had happened. She had received a phone call from an elderly woman who was looking for my grandmother. My mom said she explained that my grandmother had passed away several years ago, and the woman then wanted to know who my mother was and asked her, "Now which one of Grace's children are you?"—similar to the question that was in my dream.

My mother said that this woman sounded as if she were "calling from the grave." I tried to figure out what this all meant. The woman was just an old friend of my grandparents. It was as if I was having the dream when my mom was talking to the lady.

The one thing that did come of this was that the woman told my mom that family was so important, and that she should spend more time with her family, her brother and sister, and her children.

It was a sort of message I believe that my grandmother was trying to tell us all. She wanted us to stop our busy lives and spend more time with each other—something we all wish we had done with her before she passed away. Maybe she was trying to give us all a second chance with one another.

Now it's something I have tried to work on for several years, with hand-written letters and cards here and there, a short phone call, or e-mail to just say hello.

I still have a few dreams about events that happen or dreams of people I have not talked to in awhile. I did indeed inherit some of her special gifts, and that is her way of always contacting me even though she is not on this earth anymore. These little dreams or visions are my grandmother's way of telling me to keep in touch with certain people or that someone needs cheering up.

Dana Buchanan has been writing since she could hold a pen, making words from scribbles. She has filled notebook after notebook with her daydreams and accounts of real life, because isn't truth much better than fiction? She was blessed with a family that holds many mysteries, yet is close and supportive—a perfect combination for good storytelling. Everyone has a story to tell, no matter the topic or significance. Each story should be shared with open ears that listen to others tell their stories. You never know what mysteries might be revealed! Dana has written articles for the *Kansas City Star* and was featured in *Haunted Encounters: Personal Stories of Departed Pets*. She coordinated the school newspaper at a business school until she graduated in 1995, which included conducting interviews and research, writing an advice column and short stories, and more. She is currently working at a university and has begun attending a journalism course, where she is looking forward to learning more about writing. She hopes that everyone finds the time to communicate with those they are close to, living and dead. This world is just the beginning. May God bless you always.

My Uncle Bill

by T.J. Georgi

There are a handful of people you meet in this life who change your own absolutely. One was my great-uncle Bill.

Bill was a missionary who lived first in South America, then Spain. Being a foreign minister wasn't the easiest life to live. We knew that he'd seen the insides of more foreign jails than he would admit, all because he wanted to bring his religion to other countries, other cultures.

I didn't share Bill's or any other religion. What bonded us was the love of adventure, the magic of "what if?" Having an uncle like that sparked a curiosity in me about far-off places that continues to this day.

His visits home brought me the tang of exotic spices, a musical language, and images of snake charmers. I longed to explore the world outside my own, a fine place but a place where people often didn't travel more than a hundred miles away in a lifetime. And here was someone, in my own family, who had seen the world. He was my hero.

While back home in small-town North America, he thought nothing of talking his way out of a traffic ticket—in Spanish. His vocabulary was peppered with phrases like "And we're off, like a herd of turtles" or "He's as crazy as a ten-cent watch" or "He'll be a man before his mother." And the very un-minister-like traffic taunt: "Move, or I'll cut off your water."

His way of facing the world was pure chutzpah. He had a kind of reckless courage and an unbelievable amount of luck. There was talk about how he'd recruit young people. They came straight from the beaches and walked into his church in their swimsuits and sandy bare feet and were welcomed.

Being a minister, Bill was able to visit the local prisons to give comfort to young foreigners who found themselves on the wrong side of Spanish law and sent news of their condition home. Once, he comforted a heroin addict, the son of an American millionaire. Later they found the young man, dead, beside his diary. His last entry was about Bill's visit.

Bill would pick up any hitchhiker at any time. Inevitably, one held him up with a knife. But with his gift of a golden tongue and knowing just what people were in their hearts, Bill escaped unscathed. Each close call would create more gray hairs for his immediate family, but they knew they couldn't change him. Who, in the end, would want to?

Finally, I was able to visit him in Spain—twice. Each time he was my guide, my confidante, my pal. We shared one heart—the heart of an adventurer. On the first trip I was with my high school group. Bill would stuff as many of us into his small car as possible so that no one would be left out. Pretty soon, even students who didn't know me knew my Uncle Bill.

We rumbled along mountain roads and ate huge prawns in Spanish restaurants. I watched the dolphins play as we crossed the Strait of Gibraltar to Morocco and knew I was living the dream of my childhood. In Tangier, Bill stopped the car in front of the royal palace and casually asked us not to stare at the guards since he'd been arrested for doing that the last time he was there!

Our small group almost lost him in the maze of a Tangier souk, but found him—where else—with a snake around his neck, having charmed it right off the snake charmer. He would pick up children in the streets for a quick cuddle. It was no surprise to me to see that people treated him like the sun, just as I did.

He was Uncle Bill to the world.

One day two friends and I became hopelessly lost after a side trip on our own. At the very last bus stop there was Bill, leaning against the side of a building, waiting, as though he knew we'd be there at exactly that time.

He didn't sweat the small things in life. I think he knew that his time was running out. "Life is not just a veil of tears to be gotten through," he would say. "Life is meant to be lived."

On both of my trips he promised to take me to a mountain just outside the city where he lived. We would pass near it several times.

"It's so beautiful there," he would tell me.

But he never got the chance to show me. About a year after my last visit, Uncle Bill passed away. One of the brightest stars had fallen from my sky. That night I cried myself into an exhausted sleep.

I had a dream. In it, Bill took me to the mountain, the same one he'd been talking about during my trips. He was right—it was beautiful there. I awoke in a sea of calm.

Later I got up the courage to mention the dream to his sister, my great-aunt Eva. She was amazed. She said that she had had a similar dream. In it, Bill took her to a mountain where they used to play as children. As with me, the dream reassured her. We thought it was a nice coincidence. If Bill were trying to ease our grief from the other side, he'd succeeded. We felt at peace with his passing.

Then I mentioned something else he told me in the dream. He said he'd seen my (dead) grandmother, his sister. He had a pet name for her, one that I hadn't heard before. My great-aunt Eva said it was a childhood name they'd given their sister. She didn't know how I could possibly know about it, unless I really did have contact with my dead uncle.

Later a photo came from Spain. Uncle Bill had been laid to rest in an aboveground crypt. When I asked where it was, I found out that Bill's final resting place is on that same mountain in Spain, the one he promised to take me to one day.

And I'm sure he will.

T.J. Georgi grew up with ghost stories. She treasures the evenings spent with her extended family where the oldest, most trusted relatives would recount stories of some strange happenings and psychic predictions. How could these things be true? And yet the sources were absolutely credible. She didn't think it would ever happen to her until her deceased uncle appeared to her in a dream with words of comfort—and possible proof that there is life after death.

T.J. lives in Canada with her husband and pets, including two cats and a goldfish named Lamont.

The Furious Ghost

by Zoe Calder

We were two young girls heading up the coast of Maine into the wilds of Nova Scotia. Well, wild to us, as we had never been there before. In fact, we had never been anywhere before. Just graduated from college we were having one last summer funfest before buckling down to the "real world" of careers, paychecks, apartments, and the forced maturation those things bring. In my old but serviceable rustbucket, we'd tucked two large backpacks; a brand-new tent; borrowed sleeping bags; a good Coleman stove; a cooler that gulped ice cubes faster than the car drank gasoline; a box of food with a jar of peanut butter prominently displayed on top; flashlights; and a gigantic white jug for water, stolen from the school's lab—don't ask what had formerly been in it! We were about as happy as two free-spirited college grads can be with minimal money, a taste for adventure, and nowhere we had to be anytime soon.

That first night we camped out just inside the Maine border. I won't go into the details of trying to put up a never-before-opened tent in the dark in waist-high wet grass. But given our state of mind, the continual laughter on the ride up, the exuberance of the unknown, and our genial natures, the experience did not for one moment daunt our spirits.

Day two was as giddy and exciting as day one. We tempered our ambition, drove fewer miles, stopped more often to see the sights, and pitched our tent in late-afternoon daylight. Leslie had brought a bottle of red wine with her and we proceeded to promenade through the campgrounds looking for likely drinking buddies.

Half an hour later, we were having an impromptu party at our campsite, joined by an older couple from Alabama, two grad school guys who were headed home to Canada from Washington, D.C., and the wife of the campground owner. More wine mysteriously appeared and so did a guitar. Our sociable personalities expanded to the max as we laughed and sang the night away.

Day three dawned with some serious cirrus overhead. It wasn't raining, but would in the near future. We left our campsite, having seen none of the merrymakers of the night before. No matter. Life was easy come, easy go, carpe diem, carpe noctim (I made that last up), and on you go. Our mood remained cheery as we championed and discussed, analyzed, and dissected people, places, things, and ideas, in that order. We tired earlier than expected this day, and soon longed to stop and set up camp and rest. Besides, a light wind had sprung up along the coast and who knew when the rain would follow.

There had been no signs for campgrounds for quite a while when we spotted a large farmhouse. A man was walking down the drive to his mailbox and we pulled over without hitting him, although Leslie, who was driving, did her best. We laughed as the grim-faced man stood like a statue, mail in hand, watching us. More soberly, I rolled down the window farther and asked in my very nicest tone, "Would you happen to know of a campground nearby?"

Approaching the car, his faced softened when he saw it was just we two lambs alone on the big bad highway. "You can camp on my land, if you want," he said. We were thrilled and agreed at once. He pointed to a grassy track on the right about five hundred feet down the road. "Turn there and follow that track. Just as it gets to the ocean, it will swing right again, pass a cemetery, then peter out maybe a hundred yards beyond. You can camp there on the cliffs."

We thanked him and gingerly followed the grassy track, which wasn't as rutted as we thought it would be. When we got to the cemetery we glanced over and saw it held about forty-five graves, all ancient and all enclosed by a rusty iron picket fence.

Leslie said, "We've got to look at these graves. Think how old they must be." I agreed, and we drove on to a flat shelf of land whose lip stuck out over rocks and crashing waves fifty feet below.

Leslie parked, and I set about putting up the tent a respectable distance from the edge of the cliff. When I finished maybe fifteen minutes later, expecting that Leslie had unloaded the car, she was nowhere to be found. We had been so inseparable that it was strange not to see her. I stifled a small feeling of panic as I looked around. At my back the ocean rippled away to infinity. Directly in front of me were meadows that stretched to low hills beyond. We ought to have been able to see the highway, but it was swallowed up in the rolling fields. A group of trees in the distance marked where the farmhouse was. So far was it that I doubted anyone there could have heard us had we screamed. Not that I was planning on it. To my right the land extended in a slight downward slope to the low fences of the graveyard, then dipped out of sight. There were no houses or structures of any kind.

As I looked to my left, relief flooded me. I saw that the cliff we were on gradually eased down to the shore, and there, sitting on a piece of driftwood, was a figure that could only be Leslie. Though she had all the curves a girl could want, her overall body tended to be short and round, with saucer eyes topped off by short-cropped light brown hair on a bowling ball head. In other words, she was unmistakable.

Disturbed by Leslie's wandering away like that, I jumped up onto the back bumper of the car and hollered, "Leslie!" waving like a madwoman, but either she didn't hear me or she was ignoring me.

Cheerful, competent Leslie should have had the folding table out by now, along with our camp stove and cooler. Was she suddenly playing the princess and letting me do all the work? I felt an uncharacteristic surge of irritation. "Well," I thought, "two can play that game." I decided I'd do absolutely nothing until she returned. The tent was up and I was tired. Though normally I'm a bit afraid of heights, I walked to the edge of the cliff and looked over. In seconds I became mesmerized by the rhythm of the huge waves as they broke with flying spume and arcing streams over the boulders below. I lost all track of time as I stood there. A gust of wind made me aware that I had crept perilously close to the edge. Shuddering, I backed away.

Hating the sense of dread that had stolen upon me, I went in search of Leslie. She did not respond to my calls. She remained in a fog as I came up to her. "Leslie," I said a bit testily, "I think it might rain tonight. We ought to get started cooking." She withdrew her gaze from some evanescent world of her own and when she looked at me, she didn't appear to have fully returned from wherever her reverie had taken her. "Are you all right?" I asked, concerned. Where was my bubbly, laughing, joking friend?

"Yeah," she said, without putting much energy in the word. She got up from the sturdy piece of driftwood where she had been resting, a tree stump that had weathered itself into art, and, without giving me any recognition that would have put me at ease, started the longish walk back to camp.

As I watched Leslie shrinking into the distance, I swung myself onto the stump where she had just been sitting. It was on its side and huge roots radiated out from it at one end like a frozen Medusa head while the other end sported a serrated branch still attached to the trunk. The branch had a large cleft down the middle, with the top half bearing a deep gouge like an eye, making the whole thing resemble a shark.

The farther away Leslie got, the more uncomfortable I became. Aside from a few nosey seagulls, the only sounds were the waves piling up on shore and the wind, which had gained some strength since I last noticed it. And here I was all alone, poised between Medusa and a shark! That thought should have motivated me to leave, but somehow it didn't. I continued to sit inside the overturned stump and stare at the ocean, a foreign lassitude weakening my resolve. Once again, time vanished. A seagull swooped overhead crying, "Run! Run!" I looked up, startled. "My imagination is working overtime," I thought, but the trance was broken.

I untangled myself from the stump and headed for camp. I had come to the conclusion that this was one of those "bad vibes" places, for nothing else could explain the unlikely behavior my friend and I were indulging in. Imagine my surprise when I came upon Leslie laying in the grass having done nothing about supper. We had agreed to take turns cooking and it was her turn. Again, I felt a spurt of irritation, but this time I really noticed it. The feeling seemed imposed from the outside, not something I genuinely felt.

"Leslie, get up," I urged. She opened her eyes and blinked. I reached out my hand and she took it. Pulling her to a sitting position, I plopped down beside her. The wind whipped my ponytail to shreds while Leslie's hair stood up on end in the back.

"Listen," I said, "do you feel odd? This place is very strange and I don't like it."

Her eyes widened and she nodded. "I think this place is haunted."

Looking around uneasily, I ventured, "It's as if something has been trying to divide us or separate us."

The minute the words were out of my mouth I knew they were true. Standing, I hauled Leslie to her feet. "Let's get into the tent," I said. "Let's promise each other not to be out of the other's sight again. And I think we should leave first thing in the morning. Forget breakfast; we'll eat on the road."

Leslie nodded vigorously and asked, "What about supper?" Looking up, I saw the bright twilight had vanished. Clouds had bullied their way across the sky and now all was gray.

"Let's get into the tent," I repeated. "We can munch on some cheese and crackers."

We grabbed our water bottles and some cheddar from the cooler, and I got the crackers from the food box in the trunk. As we climbed through the tent opening, the first raindrops plummeted from the abyss of sky.

We quickly ate our meager meal, then tucked into our sleeping bags. Under the rhythmic slap of the rain on the tent roof, we soon fell asleep. I was the first to wake up. The tent was shaking as if a hand were grasping the center pole and pulling it back and forth at intervals.

"Leslie!" I hissed. "Wake up!"

"Wazzit?" she mumbled.

Taking a deep breath, I said, "Someone is shaking the tent!"

"Nah," she said. "Listen."

The wind roared overhead, then turned on a dime and splatted against the back of the tent.

"See?" she said reasonably. "It's just the wind."

But I knew it wasn't. "Leslie, no wind makes that kind of motion," I pleaded. She turned over in her sleeping bag and pulled the flap down across her head. Again, the tent was shaken violently back and forth. I could see the center pole that lay between my friend and me, tilting left and right. I had to get out of there!

"Leslie!" I shook her. "Let's get in the car."

"Mumff," she replied. "I'm staying right here. Not going out in that wind and rain."

"Well, I am," I said, feeling a sense of urgency. I pushed myself out of my bag and, dragging it with me, crawled to the tent opening. As I unzipped it, I could hardly control my fingers, so scared was I of what I might find outside. Yet I knew that staying in the tent wasn't an option. I wanted hard metal between me and whatever forces were prowling this night.

The rain attacked immediately and spared none of my near-naked body as I zipped the tent back up. I could see next to nothing, it was so dark, but a glance at the tent revealed no presence. By the time I had wide-stepped the ten feet or so to the car, my T-shirt and underpants, all I had on, were drenched. My sleeping bag had not escaped a wetting, but at least it was still dry on the inside. I wrenched the car door open, leaped into the driver's side, slammed the door shut, and locked it. I then knelt on the seat and checked the other three doors, locking them, too.

Way off in the distance my startled eyes saw lights where nothing should be. There were two, sometimes three, and they swung at treetop level, like lanterns. The more I watched them, the more impossible they became. "This cannot be happening!" I thought. "There can be no lights there. There's *nothing* there!" With my brain working heatedly, I realized no one would be out this late at night with such a storm howling so ferociously. That did it. I knew something horrible was going on and Leslie and I had become separated again. I had to get out of the car, go back to the tent, and insist she come to the car with me.

Knowing if I waited my courage would fail, I gripped the car door handle, flipped the lock, and bolted outside. An extraordinary sense of freedom overcame me as I shoved the car door closed. I felt enveloped in a time warp where everything slows down but the very center of your being. I found myself turning toward the cliff, not the tent. I strode right up to it and placed my feet on the edge. "I could leap off," I thought, "and fly!" I stood there buffeted by the wind, deluged by the rain. "What an incredible night!" I thought, shifting my feet. Toward the cemetery I heard a noise. Turning, I wondered if it was the farmer coming to check on us. And then I saw it—the barking dog, cantering in front of a large, hulking man in an old-fashioned rain slicker and flapping hat. The man held a lantern out in front of him.

"Oh," I thought, "it's the farmer." They were about fifty feet away. I took a few steps toward them. "We're fine!" I shouted. "The storm…." The words died in my throat.

The dog growled menacingly and began a leaping run. The man was now running furiously with the dog. He held up his lantern and I could see his enraged face, bloated with hate. He was no farmer! He was a sea captain, and he and his dog were headed straight for me. And I knew their intent was to push me over the cliff!

For two seconds, I froze. And then the man's arms came up, palms out, the lantern dropped to the ground, and the dog lunged viciously. I screamed and raced for the car. Once inside, I could hardly breathe. I pulled my damp sleeping bag around me and watched all the windows in turn. The storm howled and blustered, but I heard nothing else, saw no lights.

Ten minutes later I had calmed down enough to realize Leslie was still alone in the tent. Without pausing to think, I flung my sleeping bag off, opened the car door, and rushed to the tent. I got it unzipped after several fumbles, all the while yelling Leslie's name. When I darted inside, she was sitting up.

"Leslie, you've got to come into the car with me," I blurted. "Something's out there. It tried to kill me! Please!" Alarmed, she acquiesced to my panic and we streaked for the car, not bothering to zip the tent back up. She crawled into the back seat and I propped myself up in front. I told her what had happened. All she said was it must have been terrifying. Her pale face showed me she believed me. Eventually, we both fell asleep to the erratic rocking of the car.

The next morning we packed up without a word. The tent was soaked, but that was to be expected. On the way past the cemetery, Leslie insisted I stop so she could take a look at the old tombstones. I refused to get out of the car.

I watched as she wandered around from grave to grave. She paused the longest in front of the largest monument. I could see from where I sat that the date on it was 1827. A smaller stone, presumably that of a child, was set just in front. But it was not the grave of a child. When Leslie returned to the car she said in a hushed tone, "That large stone marks the burial place of a sea captain and the smaller one is for his dog. There's a whole story etched there. Both were lost on a stormy, windy night when they thought they saw a guiding light. The wind moving the tree branches made the light appear to be from a swinging lantern leading them to the safety of a cove. Instead, they were pulled onto the rocks and drowned."

"And now he wants to take everyone else with him!" I said vehemently. "Well, not this girl! Let's get out of here!"

It wasn't until hours later that it occurred to me to wonder: How did they know—those gravestone etchers—what had happened?

Zoe Calder is a teacher of writing, literature, and speech. Her photography, short stories, poems, and articles have been published in numerous newspapers and magazines. She lives by the ocean in Maine.

My Beneficent Ghost

by Claire Bocardo

My husband's death from melanoma in 1997 should not have come as a shock; he had endured three surgeries and six months of interferon treatment to defeat it. But I was born a determined and incurable optimist, so when several exams after the last surgery showed no more cancer, I believed he'd beaten it.

Then one late October night, while watching TV after supper, Larry said he was dizzy, so I helped him to the couch to lie down. He tried to tell me more, but he couldn't form the words. Thinking "stroke," I called 911. By the time the team arrived five minutes later, he couldn't talk. We took him to the hospital, and soon after he arrived he started having seizures. They put him on a respirator, shot him full of paralytics to control the seizures, and took him upstairs for a closer look.

Sitting on a bench in the hall while they conducted the scan, I felt his presence. Had it been my first such experience, I might have thought I was out of my mind with fear and grief. But when my grandmother had died thirty years before in California, she'd come to Texas to bless me on her way home.

I'd been watering my roses when I was suddenly enveloped in her body scent, an unmistakable mix of Cashmere Bouquet powder and old-lady sweat. I stood still, waiting to see what would happen next, and then was suffused with a feeling of total and absolute love. The next day, my mother called to tell me Grandma had died at just that moment.

And eight years earlier, when Larry had nearly died from a bleeding ulcer, I'd left him at the hospital after they'd said I couldn't see him for several hours. On my way back, the car filled with his scent. Startled and scared, I blurted out, "Don't you dare die on me now! We've just got to the easy part!" When I got back to the hospital, he had begun to recover.

This time, I knew beyond question that he was taking his leave.

Please don't go until the kids have come and gone, I thought to him. *They need to say good-bye, and they're on their way.*

They arrived, and all seven of us were allowed to be with him in the ER while we waited for the results. The scan showed that a brain tumor had been building silently for months. It had burst, and the pressure had destroyed his brain; surgery was pointless. But because of the drugs they'd given him, the law required that he be kept alive for twelve more hours. I arranged to spend the night with him in the Intensive Care Unit, and by the time we arrived there, someone had brought in a reclining chair for me.

It's OK now, I told him. *Everybody's gone. You're free to go.*

At about half-past three, I finally unwound enough to sit in that chair. I leaned back, closed my eyes, and was immediately plunged into a vast, black void with a single point of light above, like a star, and an overwhelming sense of "lostness."

Don't wander around in the dark, Sweetheart, I said. *Go to the light.*

The nurse had been coming in every few minutes to pull the hairs on his legs for a pain reaction. The next time she came in, he was gone.

On the night before Larry's funeral, I was riding in the back of my daughter's car when I heard in my mind, *I know, Sweetheart. I love you too*, and I knew he was with me once again. From then on, he was present almost all the time for several months.

For the first month or two—because, he said, he'd gone so suddenly that he hadn't had time to say proper good-byes—he gave family members little "experience gifts." Our son-in-law, who'd been trying to find the right new job for about a year, found the perfect one two weeks after Larry's exit. One son he'd played golf with had an eagle on the hole where we'd planted a tree with Larry's ashes under it.

He came in a dream to our gambling daughter-in-law and gave her a winning number. And on what would have been Larry's sixtieth birthday, our youngest son, an aspiring jazz bassist, wandered into the Blue Note Café in New York City on open mike night and wound up on stage, keeping up with Roy Hargrove and other jazz greats. That was no coincidence: It was Larry who'd taught our kids to love jazz.

One night, after a particularly hard day, I lay in bed weeping and talking to him.

"I'm so grateful that you come to me this way," I said, "but I miss your touch." I felt his hand cup the back of my head and give it a little shake, a gesture of affection he'd made as long as I'd known him.

At first, I was simply numb with shock. That ended on Christmas night, when I was plunged into a grief so deep I thought I might follow him. I still don't know how I'd have come through it without his presence to guide and comfort me. In February, I had two life-threatening accidents in two weeks, and he scolded me for my carelessness.

"You can't come here now," he said. "You're not done there yet." I already knew that, of course, but it forced me to understand that I couldn't go on just existing; I had to make a conscious decision to live.

After the first deep grief had passed he came less often, but his gifts to me kept coming.

I had always wanted to live in the country, but Larry could never even contemplate living outside the city limits. "One of these days," he would say, "they're going to carry me out of this house by the handles, and then you can go anywhere you want." I had planned to postpone any big changes for at least a year, but within weeks of his death, at his constant urging, I began scouring the countryside for land on which to build my farmhouse.

I was looking for about five acres within thirty miles of our home, but I found that if I bought land that close I couldn't afford to build on it. So I kept going farther and farther away until, one April day, I found fourteen acres fifty miles from home. A virgin prairie hillside covered in wildflowers, with a creek at the bottom, it was so serenely beautiful that the first time my foot touched its soil every cell in my body said, "Aa-aah!" Torn with indecision I went to see it three times in a single week. Then, driving home from the last visit, I sensed Larry in the car with me.

I don't know, honey, I thought. *It's too big and too far away, but it's so lovely... What do you think?*

It was one of the very few times I heard actual words, instead of simply sensing his meaning.

Hell, Claire, I'm no judge of land—you know that! All I want is for you to be happy. Is this going to make you happy?

Well, it'll help.

Then buy it!

So the next problem was where to find the down payment. A day or two later, when I went to the safe to look for something else, I was surprised to find a three-inch stack of U.S. Savings Bonds that more than covered it.

I put our house up for sale and started planning the new one. House-planning had been my lifelong hobby, and I had already drawn a house I thought was perfect, but it wouldn't fit on the land I'd bought. I created several more designs and then, still dissatisfied, dug out ten years' worth of house-plan magazines for new ideas.

The very first one fell open to a passive solar plan with strong possibilities. I ordered the plans and then modified them extensively to fit my own needs, making the engineering notes useless. Along with the passive solar technology, I planned to use only salvaged, recycled, or renewable materials. Besides using unusual materials and technology, the fan-shaped design was full of odd angles and personal quirks.

Now, with only a floor plan and the materials specifications I'd written to go by, I needed a builder for my unique little house. I sent fifteen bid packages to local builders and received only one positive response; the rest wanted to build "little boxes," get paid, and get out.

But the one man who did feel able to build it from only a floor plan was just the sort of man whom Larry might have chosen for me: an honest, reputable contractor, clever and creative, who lived only about a mile from my property. He even had a little apartment on his place—with a fenced yard for my dogs—that he was willing to rent to me until my house was built. Living so close to the project, I was able to be on site nearly every day to make decisions, and we made the house up as we went along.

As the project progressed, Larry came to me less and less frequently, but he was always there when I needed him. While he had no opinions on questions of style, he helped with financial choices. For example, I wanted wood-framed windows instead of vinyl or aluminum, but they were twice the cost. I agonized over that for weeks until Larry stopped me.

You're going to be looking out those windows every day for the rest of your life, he said. *If they're not right, they'll spoil the house for you. Get the windows you want.* I did.

I moved into the house around Thanksgiving of 1999, when he'd been gone just over two years. There was still no floor in the living area; I'd designed a wood-and-poured-concrete floor and planned to make it myself, but then realized that I lacked both the know-how and the physical strength. With the house almost finished, I couldn't find anybody to create that floor for me. Then, through another much-too-tidy "accident," I met a man who was both able and willing to do it.

The floor was finished during the first week of January. I hadn't heard from Larry since I'd moved in and thought he had stopped coming, but about a week later I felt his presence in the car. He wanted to know how I was doing.

I still miss you, I told him, *and I'll probably keep on missing you until I come to join you. But I'm all right, honey; I'm happy.*

I felt a sense of blessing, and then he was gone.

I've heard it said that people who have died suddenly sometimes stay around until they're sure their work is done, and my experience with Larry supports that idea. Larry seemed to feel that his "work" included seeing me established in my new life. Once satisfied, he was able to go on to his.

When we were very young and couldn't afford life insurance, I once heard him tell a friend, "My responsibility has to end somewhere, and death is as good a place as I can think of." I'm enormously grateful that he changed his mind.

Claire Bocardo grew up in Washington State. She met and married Larry at San Diego State College (now University) in 1959 and moved to Texas four years later. They had four children, three of whom still live in the Plano, Texas, area; the fourth is a musician in New York City. After Larry's death, she moved to a four-teen-acre plot near Tom Bean, Texas, in the Red River Valley. She now has six grandchildren and a new great-grand-daughter. Claire is the author of four novels—*Maybe Later, Love*; *Sweet Nothings*; *Lovers and Friends*; and *Becoming Sarah*—all available at www.wings-press.com.

Ghost from the Future

by Lyn Coffin

I was a hospice social worker, and Dorothea was one of my long-term patients. Dorothea was in her eighties, and dying of chronic obstructive pulmonary disease. During one of our last interviews, Dorothea told me that she had always wanted to see a psychic and regretted never having done so. I pointed out that it wasn't too late, and asked if she would like me to get her the name of a respected psychic in the area. She said she would, and I called her that evening with the name and phone number.

When I next saw Dorothea, two weeks later, she told me how grateful she was to me for the contact. She had been to the psychic, and felt the psychic was "right on the money." She asked if I would like to hear the tape the psychic had made of their interview together. I said yes. Proudly, Dorothea put on the tape and we sat there in her kitchen, listening. On the tape, the psychic said what I would have said about Dorothea, put into "psychic" instead of "social work" terms. She said Dorothea had lived a long life and had her emotional affairs in good order. She spoke about Dorothea's good relationship with her living family (her daughter) and her deceased family—father, mother, and older brother. She said Dorothea had really "no unfinished business."

As I listened to the psychic, I at first heard nothing with which I could not wholeheartedly agree. Dorothea had been in hospice therapy with me for a number of months and she did

94

seem to have her emotional house in order. She had talked to me about her somewhat distant mother, her reconciliation with her older brother, the many happy times she had spent with her father. Whatever small traumas she had suffered in her childhood seemed to be resolved and safely in the past.

But as the psychic kept talking, the hairs on the back of my neck began to rise, and I suddenly saw a ghost. I don't know what else to call her. This was not the sheeted and "whoo whoo" ghost of Halloween stories. This was the ghost of a little girl. Not only did I see a ghost, but I also saw her surroundings. I seemed to have been transported in time and place. I was floating above the second landing of a stairwell carpeted in green. There was a window to my left through which streamed the early morning sun. Outside was a large Douglas fir. I could count the steps leading up to the landing.

The "ghost" just ahead of and a few feet below me was the ghost of a little girl of about five, facing up the final short flight of stairs. I couldn't see her face, but I saw her short and puff-sleeved red dress, and the scuffs on the back of her black patent leather shoes. I saw her wheat-blonde, shoulder-length hair.

And I saw her pale, thin arms held slightly out from her sides; I saw her small, tightly clenched fists. Even seen from the back, I knew this ghost child was both terrified and furious.

She was staring up at the second-floor landing. She wasn't making a sound (I was aware of small birds chattering in the fir tree) but I could "hear" her soundless tears. I knew she was furious at someone in her family. A male. Her father or her brother. Her father.

I knew something terrible had just happened.

And then I knew what it was. A shot had just gone off. I heard it backward. I knew, this little ghost of a girl knew, that her father, her doomed, beloved father, had just shot and killed himself. Her father had been the love at the heart of her life, and now he was gone.

As if sensing my presence, the girl turned around, and a small Dorothea looked up at me, her face wet with tears. For a second, she seemed to see me. I tried to "send her" my love.

The connection faded almost immediately, but not before I realized that I was the one from another time period; I was the one floating above the floor; I was the ghost.

The realization returned me suddenly to my "normal" present: I was back in the kitchen. Dorothea asked me for my reaction. Didn't I think what the psychic had said was 100 percent on the money?

But I knew now, somehow, that what the psychic had said was wrong in some fundamental way: I knew that both the psychic and I had missed a key fact of Dorothea's childhood and the state of her soul: There was much work yet to be done, and not much time.

But Dorothea had shared so many "happy" memories with me, most of them of her father. Was what she had told me a lie? Was what I had seen a lie?

I didn't want to upset Dorothea, but I had never fibbed to her before, and this didn't seem like the time to start. When she asked me a second time whether I agreed with the psychic, I said no. I told her what I had seen, all of it—her as a terrified and angry little girl on the stairway, and me floating above her, a ghost from the future. Dorothea turned completely pale, and called to her daughter in a panicky voice, "Helen! Helen! Come here!" When Helen ran in from the living room, Dorothea told me— commanded me, really—"Tell her what you saw." Obediently, I described the stairway scene. Now it was Helen's turn to become pale.

When I'd finished, Dorothea asked Helen, "Should I tell her?"

"You might as well," Helen said. "She already seems to know."

Dorothea told me that the man she had described so lovingly as her father was really her stepfather. Her biological father had shot himself to death when she was five. Her first memory was of being on the green carpeted stairs and hearing the shot—knowing instinctively, intuitively, what he had done, feeling a great sense of anger, and a greater sense of loss.

Dorothea and I set to our therapeutic work, processing her unresolved feelings about her beloved father's suicide. She died peacefully about three weeks later.

Now, when I hear people talking about the ghosts they've seen, I want to say, "Sometimes ghosts can be from the future, not the past—I know, because I was one."

Lyn Coffin's most recent book, *Crystals of the Unforeseen: A Book of Women's Voices (Poetry, Fiction and Drama)* was published by Plain View Press. She is the author of two previous books of poetry—*The Poetry of Wickedness* (Ithaca House) and *Human Trappings* (Abattoir Editions)—and four books of translation. One of her fictions appeared in *Best American Short Stories 1979*.

She's won grants from the Michigan Council of the Arts and NEH. Her plays have been performed semi-widely in Michigan, and she has published poetry, fiction, and non-fiction in over fifty small magazines, as well as *Catholic Digest* and *Time*.

The Academy of American Poets awarded her first prize in a translation competition judged by William Meredith, and while she was at the University of Michigan, Lyn won Major/Minor Hopwoods in every category. She competed at the 1998 National Poetry Slam in Austin, Texas.

Lyn's dramas have been performed on radio and television. Her play *Tonsils and Adenoids* was a finalist in an Actor's Theatre of Louisville short play competition.

Lyn was an editor of *The Michigan Quarterly Review*, and a member of the Purple Rose Playwriting Lab, one of five playwrights involved in its PAD Lab. Lyn was active in Michigan Playwrights, Ann Arbor Playwrights, and Detroit Women Writers, and was a poetry columnist for AOL's PoetryList.

This year, Lyn launched Hugo House's "Writers and Work" series, and performed at Bumbershoot. She has a story forthcoming in *Golden Handcuffs*, and is a WITS writer at Renton High School.

She does online writing consultation and can be reached via www.projectstory.com/lyncoffin.

Father's Passing

by Sybil Simon

I have always been open to fleeting glimpses of the super-natural. There was the ghost cat that appeared in the garage of my last home. As a child I often heard footsteps coming up the stairs in the middle of the night. They would awaken me and I'd huddle in my bed, quaking in fear. What happened the September of my father's death, however, will stay with me the rest of my life.

In 1992 I was recently divorced, and living in an apartment in California. I worked a demanding middle management job for which I traveled frequently. Before my divorce, I would try to make a trip to Baltimore at least once a year to visit with my family. As Labor Day approached, my younger sister phoned to fill me in on what was happening in my hometown.

"You should come home for Labor Day. We're having family over for a barbecue. Randy just bought a spiffy new gas grill. It's been over a year since you were here last," she admonished.

"Closer to two," I admitted.

"Mom noticed you missed coming last year. You know how she is. She keeps ranting on about California and the hippies and liberals there."

I probably sighed at this point. I know I looked at my calendar because I found myself on a plane to Baltimore five weeks later. I remember I had to adjust my schedule at work to accommodate the trip and ended up piggybacking it with a convention I had to attend in Chicago.

My sister May met me at the airport luggage turnstile. She was wearing a jaunty pantsuit, Mickey Mouse embossed on the denim shirt, a matching image running down her right leg. We hugged as we normally did after so many months of separation. The hug tossed May's matching denim cap on the floor of the terminal. (May is a hat person). We both bent down to retrieve it at the same time, bumping heads, which made us giggle.

"It's good to see you, Syb," May said after the fit of laughter.

"Yes, it's been too long."

My luggage finally popped out and tumbled to the conveyor belt. We attempted to pull it off as it came around. The crowd pulsed about us, but May was persistent. "I got it," she said.

"I do, too." Between the two of us, we managed to wrestle it off the belt and onto the floor of the terminal. The luggage had wheels and a handle that pulled out. I got the handle in the right position and followed May out the door.

That night, we barbecued on May and Randy's deck. The mosquitoes were biting with fury. At one point, I went inside and rummaged though my luggage for repellant. I brought it out for the others, and we sprayed ourselves liberally. May got some citronella candles and lit them, prompting the mosquitoes to lessen their attack. We enjoyed our burgers and talked about Randy's recent promotion. He worked for the fire department and was just promoted to fire chief.

The next morning we had breakfast and left the house about 9 a.m. for the short drive to our parents' house. Mom greeted us at the door and I remember thinking how much she had aged since I'd last seen her. Dad, on the other hand, looked great. We hugged and, while my sister and mother sat with a cup of coffee at the kitchen table, I followed Dad to the basement. The basement had always been my dad's sanctuary. The stone house had a little storefront at street level where, for years, my father would open for business on weekends, repairing watches for neighbors and friends. Since his retirement, he had used the old store to tinker in. Evidence of his most recent project was scattered across the counter of the store. He was taking apart an old table clock; wheels and parts littered the glass.

"You've always been fascinated with clocks and watches," I remember telling him.

A strange looked crossed his face. "Time is so elusive, Syb. We think we can measure it. We invent instruments to do that but, even without watches and clocks, time marches on."

I'll never forget those words or many of the other things he said that morning. At one point in the conversation, he mentioned my mother. He seemed concerned that he would pass away, and May would be out of town on business, and I would be far away in California. I don't remember what I said to try to reassure him, only that it was the most strangely intimate conversation I had ever had with my father.

After several hours of visiting, May mentioned that we should be going. The next day was the Labor Day barbecue and we needed to make a run to the grocery store. As we walked down the stairs to the pavement, I glanced over at the shop window. Below the sign that hung there—Edward T. Barr, Master Watchmaker—I could see my father's head bent over his clock parts, tinkering.

That evening, in May's guest room, I tossed and turned, my father's words tumbling around in my head. Shortly before midnight, I turned on the bedside lamp and pulled a paperback out of my luggage. I read for a little over an hour until I began to feel sleepy. Turning off the lamp, I lay back against the pillow and drifted into a fitful sleep.

How long I slept I cannot say. I awakened on my back, then opened my eyes only slightly. Something misty was floating at the foot of my bed and I opened my eyes wider. The apparition looked like my father, but at a much younger age. His hair was blond, full, and wavy the way I remembered him when I was a young child. His clothes—what I could make out of them—looked like the work clothes he used to wear to his job. He lifted his right hand and pointed to a watch strapped to his left wrist. Suddenly, he was gone. I think at that point I convinced myself it was only a dream. I turned over on my stomach and fell back to sleep.

May's pounding at the bedroom door awakened me. "Syb, you awake?"

"I am now," I said. I flipped over in bed as she poked her head into the room. I glanced over at the travel alarm I'd brought with me. It was nearly 6 a.m.

"Mom just called. It's Daddy. She thinks he's dead. He isn't breathing. Last night he slept on the floor because his back was bothering him. She got up to go to the bathroom a little after 2 and noticed he wasn't snoring. Damn! I don't know what I'm feeling right now." May walked over and sat on the bed.

I reached over to comfort her. My mind was in turmoil as I remembered the misty profile I thought I'd seen early that morning. Dad's conversation from the day before came back to me.

"Mom's been sitting on the bed for hours just staring at him and praying the rosary."

I let this sink in. "I should get dressed. We need to get over there."

"Randy called 911. Get dressed quickly. You know how Mom is—she'll freak if the police get there before we do."

The rest of the day is a blur to me. I remember we got there at the same time as the police. May and I spent a good part of the day calling relatives. I had to cancel my return flight home and stay a lot longer than intended. The airline was helpful and rebooked me without a charge. I have never told May about the vision I'd had that Labor Day morning, but I did tell her about the conversation I'd had with our father. At the end of that long day, I retired to May's guest room and wrote it all down in a travel journal I used to take along on my trips. This account is from the words I wrote on Labor Day, September 7, 1992, the day of my father's passing.

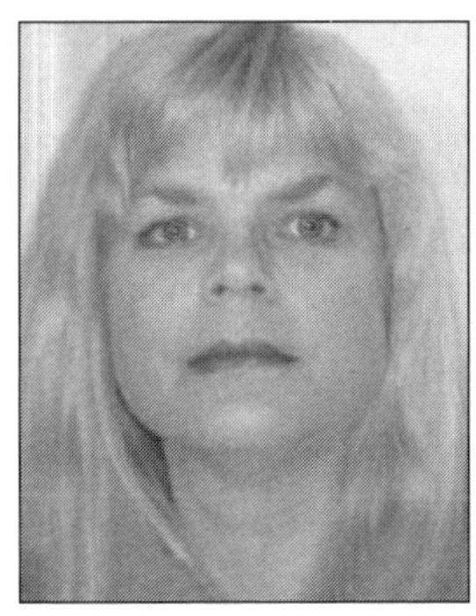

Sybil Simon is a full-time writer living near Fort Worth, Texas, with her husband and their eight cats. She has always loved to write. Since her childhood, Sybil has had unusual visits from entities she can only call ghostly. A combination of her unearthly experiences and her love of writing has directed her muse to speculative fiction—horror and fantasy.

Sybil is a member of several online writing groups including The Horror Writer's Association. When she is not writing or cleaning out litter pans, Sybil likes to shop for antiques and visit old cemeteries where she ruminates over gravestones.

Mother Love

by Ginnie Siena Bivona

My mother had her first operation for breast cancer when she was forty. I was fifteen, and completely unable to comprehend the suffering she must have experienced. Moms aren't supposed to be that sick. Moms aren't supposed to lie in bed all day in a darkened room. Friends and relatives pitched in until she managed to get through the chemo and radiation. My solution to the whole thing was to pretend that it wasn't happening.

And of course, in those days, that was the accepted way to handle serious problems. One simply walked around them, studiously looking the other way. No matter what the elephant in the living room looked like, how big and ugly it was, one simply did not acknowledge that it almost filled the room. The terrible word "cancer" was never said out loud. There were whispers and sympathetic sighs, but the "c" word was not mentioned.

After a while, she got better and our lives, at least in my young eyes, returned to almost normal. We sang when we did the dishes, and I helped with the laundry and dusting. Nothing changed. Sometimes, if she were dressing to go somewhere, she would send me down into the basement to bring her "other side" up from the clothesline. We laughed about it, and once I remember stuffing it down the front of my shirt, right in the middle. One big boob, poking straight out in front. Since I really didn't have all that much in the way of bosoms, we both thought it was hilarious.

When I was eighteen the cancer came back, and she had to have the other breast removed. That's when it stopped being funny. We moved out of the house I had grown up in because she could no longer care for it. The new apartment was way out on the outskirts of Cleveland, and I had to take a Greyhound bus to my job at a university school of dentistry. It was time for me to begin looking for a husband, and an educated man was, of course, preferred. It was the perfect job.

My dad hired a woman to come in and clean because Mom couldn't do it any more. She was sick all the time, constantly going to the doctor, and was usually in a depressed mood. My parents had never gotten along very well to begin with, and my dad avoided the problem by staying at work all the time. That left me to talk to Mom, and do my best to cheer her up. And I did just that. I played the good little girl, always popping around, acting gay and silly, trying to make my mother smile.

Then she went back to the hospital again. And one night, when I had just turned twenty-one and was getting ready to go on a date, my father told me to come sit down. He needed to talk to me.

"She's not going to get well," he said. " She has maybe six to nine months… that's all." I was stunned. And slipped immediately into disbelief. Of course she would get well. Those stupid doctors were always crying wolf. Moms don't die. They live forever.

When she came home from the hospital I had to learn how to give her pain shots. Sometimes in the middle of the night, I would become so annoyed at having to get up again, prepare the needle, sterilize the area, and make sure the medicine was not going into a vein, which occasionally happened and meant starting over from the beginning. I never let her know, I thought, but now as an adult, and a mother myself, I am certain she sensed it.

The illness dragged on. Life became routine, almost bearable. I was twenty-one and it was time for me to get serious about my future. I wouldn't date anyone who wasn't eligible; that meant educated, religious, and wanting lots and lots of children. Friends started bringing around young men who fit the requirements.

It didn't take long, and by the time I neared my twenty-second birthday, I met the perfect one. Within weeks we were in love. Sometimes, when Mom felt well enough, as soon as I got home from a date, she would get up so that I could tell her all about my evening. She was so happy. At last her little daughter would be married. The ultimate goal of every young woman in those days. It almost seemed to give her new life too.

One night, after a date with my newfound love, I came home and jubilantly announced that he and I were going to get married, probably in August.

"So soon?" she gasped. "That's too soon!"

I knew in my heart that she was staying alive only to see me married, and I had just pronounced her death sentence. Angrily I said, "Fine, then! We'll wait until after Christmas, right after the first of the year!"

We set the date for January 30th. I had to plan my own wedding because by that time she was much too ill to do anything. My aunt, my mother's sister, was angry at me for getting married when my mother was so desperately sick, but she didn't understand that I wanted my mom at my wedding, and she wanted to be there. We were doing what we both wanted most.

The wedding went off nicely. It was a small affair, with friends and family coming back to the apartment for a short reception after the church service. I looked beautiful. My mom sat, like a queen, in a high-backed chair and she never stopped smiling once.

After the wedding we went to the mountains for our honeymoon, and then to our new apartment in a small town in Indiana, where my spouse had his first job out of college.

I called home every other day, and Mom sounded fine. She said she was fine. Weak, but still OK. I stopped worrying.

Then, on February 25th my dad called. Mom was back in the hospital, and it did not look good. I needed to come home. I took the first train out the next day and went straight from the train station to the hospital. The doctor told me that there was no hope, and that they had put my mother in a private room to await the end.

It took a long time. I was alone in the room with her, on March 4th, late on a cold snowy afternoon, when her long slow dance with death ended. I was terrified. The death throes were dreadful, agonizing, and I stood in paralyzed horror watching my mother's contorted face as she fought off the inevitable.

Then it was over. At the funeral everybody hovered over me, the poor little new bride with no mother. I felt as cold as the snow that covered the ground. I don't think, after that first night, I cried again through the whole awful affair.

When I finally got back to my home, to my husband, and to my new life, I cried then. But the worst part was that I could not recall my mother's face, except in those twisted and tortured last few moments. I would take out snapshots and look at them, but the face that haunted me was the one I saw in the hospital. I could not shake it from my mind.

A long time later, perhaps a year, I woke, startled, from a deep sleep one night, and there at the foot of my bed stood my mother. There was a tall green hedge behind her, like the one in our backyard, and she had on one of those tacky housedresses women wore in those days. She had a nice white apron on, too. A little "rounded" (she was never skinny), a few hairs straying down on her forehead. It was my mom. Exactly the way she always looked. She smiled at me. The most incredible smile. It radiated joy, well-being, and happiness, so much so, that even as a writer of some experience, I have not the words to describe how glorious she looked.

"Oh," I thought, "I had no idea my mother was so beautiful!"

And then it was over. She was gone.

Since then, I can only recall how my mom looked at that moment. On several occasions I have been told it was my imagination, a way of dealing with her death. But I have never doubted that it really was my mother, coming back to comfort her beloved child. And now I know, for a fact, that moms do live forever, after all.

Books have been a passion for Ginnie Siena Bivona since the very first day she first learned that those marks on a piece of paper told a story. She has never been without a book close at hand ever since. Now, as an older person (we won't say *how* old), she is amazed and delighted to discover that she is a writer, and even more wonderfully, a publisher of books. Life is full of great surprises. She is the author of several cookbooks and a novel—*Ida Mae Tutweiler and The Traveling Tea Party*—and one of the founders of Atriad Press. She lives in Dallas, Texas, where she shares her life with five adult children and seven very nearly perfect grandchildren.

A Few Words

by Stephen D. Rogers

I woke from a dream to see my grandfather standing at the foot of my bed. He smiled and said, "I liked what you said at the church today." Each of his grandchildren had been asked to say a few words.

"I couldn't begin to summarize your life, to describe your importance to me."

"Writing a story which tied together so many of my interests was clever. Funny too."

"I'm glad you weren't offended. After the ceremony, several people told me it was a fitting tribute. Jack said he finally realized what you saw in *Star Trek*."

"I know."

"Mom always said I took after you. I was so disappointed when I didn't grow to your imposing height."

He laughed. "We are similar in many ways."

"I left a copy of my first book with you to read. You never said what you thought."

"I was impressed."

"Why didn't you ever tell me? If anyone could understand how I felt, could appreciate the mathematical motifs, it would be you. I waited and waited for you to say something about the manuscript and now it's too late."

"No, it isn't. We're talking now, aren't we?"

He had a point. "This is probably more words than we ever exchanged while you were still alive."

"I was always there, watching, following your achievements and setbacks. It may not have seemed as though I was paying attention but I was."

"I was paying attention too. That's how I was able to put together the story I read at the church today. A story isn't a relationship. It's a performance which I would happily trade for memories."

My grandfather shifted. "Do you know what brought me my happiest moments?"

"Playing music? Mathematics? The television shows you discovered in reruns after you retired?"

"You children. I missed the childhood of my own children. In those days, fathers didn't become involved. Besides, I was too busy working multiple jobs to put food on the table. You children gave me a second chance at happiness."

"I never knew."

He shrugged. "I'm a man of few words."

"I know. We're alike that way."

We spent the next few minutes in a comfortable silence.

Our silences had always been comfortable, but what exactly did that leave me now that he was gone? Remember the time he sat in his chair and I sat on the couch? Remember the time we both sat at the dining room table? Remember the time I looked through his tools while he worked on the organ?

"What are you thinking?"

Now it was my turn to laugh. I did take after him, me and my introspective silences. "I was thinking about the things we never said."

"Such as?"

I took a deep breath. "When I first learned I was going to talk today, I wished I had some significant anecdote to share. Advice you'd given me. Encouragement. Words of wisdom."

"Why do you think I had any answers?"

"You'd lived almost ninety years. Every decision I needed to make, you'd already made. Every path I walked down alone, you'd done so before me."

"There was no shortage of people in our family willing to tell you what to do."

"But they weren't me."

"Neither am I."

"No, but you were close. We're alike enough that your insights would have been valuable, your experiences similar to my own. What did you think when I dropped out of college? You were a learned man, a professor. You must have had an opinion."

"You never asked."

"I'm asking now."

"You did what you felt you had to do."

"That's not a personal response. You could be describing anything I've ever done, what anybody in the world has ever done. What did it mean to you that I, your flesh and blood, dropped out of school?"

"What difference does it make? Only you live your own life. Ultimately, yours is the only opinion that matters."

"That's not an answer."

"Life is not a piece of music where a wrong note jars the ear, a mathematical proof where one misstep causes the logic to unravel. Life does not have an organized structure, an internal truth against which our decisions can be judged right or wrong."

I wanted to jump from the bed, force him to talk. "You're spouting theory. I'm asking for particulars."

"Are you?"

I stopped myself from replying too quickly. Was I really looking for his honest opinion? If so, why? He was right in saying that I was the one who had to live my life and that's the way I'd lived it. Why then was I bemoaning the lack of advice that I probably wouldn't have followed? Was I only hoping for approval, forgiveness?

"I'm not sure."

My grandfather nodded. "After walking the earth for almost ninety years, the one thing I can tell you with any certainty is that there are no easy answers."

I sat quietly for a moment. Then I started. "No, that's not true. There are some answers that are easy. You may not know what I should have done but you do know your response to what I did."

He simply looked at me. Finally, he spoke. "I have to go."

"That's not fair. This is the first time we've ever really talked and you still haven't answered my question. Stop! Don't go yet—"

He shimmered for a second and then he was gone.

I woke from a dream to turn off the alarm clock. Sitting there in bed, rubbing my eyes, I remembered an earlier dream, a conversation with my dead grandfather. It had been a dream, of course, because it couldn't have been anything else.

Then I saw the last present he'd made me, two pieces of wood hinged together to simulate a box—"For the man who wants nothing." It was sitting there next to the alarm clock, far from the shelf where I kept it, giving my grandfather the chance to have the last word without even speaking.

He'd answered me after all.

While Stephen Rogers worked at John Stone's Inn in Ashland, Massachusetts, he never saw the three ghosts who reside there. He can be contacted through www.stephendrogers.com.

The Phantom Milkman

by Greg Faherty

Growing up in Stony Point, New York, a suburb of Manhattan, I was familiar with a variety of ghost stories and legends. Mad Anthony Wayne, the Spook Rock ghost, haunted houses, and many more stories abounded in the region, some dating back to before the Revolutionary War. However, my first encounter with an actual ghost was a relatively unknown spirit. It happened one summer night when I was about ten years old.

I was spending the night at a friend's house, a boy that lived down the street from me. There were four of us having a sleepover that night—Rich, Johnny, Billy, and myself. We had originally intended to spend the night in the wooden "fort" we had recently built in the woods behind Rich's house, but heavy rains had forced us to alter our plans and stay inside the house. In the comfort of Rich's room we spent most of the night talking, reading comic books, and munching on an assortment of chips and snack foods. Like most boys our age, we had every intention of staying up for the entire night, but eventually we all drifted off to sleep sometime after midnight.

It was at least two or three hours later when Johnny woke us up in an excited voice. "C'mere, guys, you have to see this!" Johnny was standing by the window, looking outside. Struggling out from under the covers of our various blankets and sleeping bags, we all rushed over to the window. There we saw a sight that most people wouldn't believe.

Rich's window faced the backyard, and beyond that, the woods that at the time stretched from Tompkins Cove to Stony Point, paralleling Cricketown Road and ending at Heights Road. The woods were separated from Rich's backyard by a low stone wall, and approximately 50 feet beyond that was a large hard-packed dirt path that began at Heights Road and extended all the way to Wayne Avenue in Tompkins Cove. In those days children of all ages used the path to play on and as a shortcut to friends' houses. Years previously, it had been one of only three roads bridging the two towns.

Now, as we stared in wonder, something else was using the path we all referred to as the "dirt road." A glowing figure was slowly making its way down the path, heading southeast toward Heights Road. This figure was not traveling on foot, but rather driving a horse-drawn cart. Through the light mist left behind by the rain we could clearly see the horse and its driver. Horse, driver, and cart all glowed a pale green, seeming to shimmer slightly in the mist, as though surrounded by some type of shifting aura. The driver appeared to be an elderly black man, dressed in jeans and a flannel shirt. Through the open window the muted clip-clop of the horse's hooves came back to us, as well as the tinny jingle of the metal on leads and the creaking of the four wheels of the flat cart pulled by the horse, upon which the driver sat on his slightly raised seat.

As we watched in stunned silence, the horse and cart rolled slowly along the path, the driver looking neither left nor right. We could see boxes or crates of some type piled in the cart. With wondering eyes we followed the progress of the cart as it moved past Rich's property and then behind the house next door. Soon after that we lost sight of it as it moved behind some trees, but we could still hear the sounds of the ghostly horse and its cart for a few minutes more.

The disappearance of the cart seemed to break the spell that had held us motionless. We all started talking excitedly at once, asking each other if we really saw what we thought we had seen, what was it, should we tell Rich's parents, should we go outside and look for it. There was no doubt in our minds that we had seen a ghost or spirit. One of the nice things about being a child is that immediate acceptance of things supernatural or unexplainable.

Rich interrupted our babbling voices, hissing at us to be quiet. "Shh! You'll wake up my parents! Be quiet for a minute and let's figure out what to do."

"I say we follow it!" said Johnny. "If we go out there now, we can catch up to it on the path."

"And then what?" asked Billy. "I don't want run up behind a ghost. What if we make it mad?"

We decided that Johnny and I would go out in the yard up to the stone wall, and look down the path to see if we could still see it. If we could, we would signal Rich and Billy, and all of us would follow it. Johnny and I quickly got dressed and quietly snuck out of the house and sped across the backyard. Standing on top of the low wall, we looked down the path in the direction the apparition had traveled. We could see for a distance of about two or three houses, but there was no sign of our spirit visitor. We returned to the house and the four of us sat down on the floor in Rich's room to decide our next move.

"It stopped raining," I said. "That could be important."

"Why?" queried Billy.

"I know," answered Rich. "That means that anything walking or driving on that dirt road will have left tracks in the mud, and if it doesn't rain anymore tonight then the tracks will still be there in the morning."

"Right!" I said. "All we have to do is stay awake tonight, and watch to see if it rains again. Then, as soon as it's light out, we can go back there and see if there are tracks in the mud. If there are, then whatever we saw was alive and real. If not, then we know it was a ghost."

We decided to stay up the rest of the night in pairs. We used rock, paper, scissors to choose who had to stay up. Rich and Johnny ended up being the two chosen. Billy and I went to sleep. You might think that it would have been impossible to go back to sleep after what we had seen, but I drifted off almost immediately.

The next morning we were all dressed and outside before anyone else in the house was awake. We ran into the woods to look at the path. One glance told us all we needed to know—no tracks! We really were dealing with a ghost. We walked the entire length of the dirt road, almost two miles, and didn't find so much as a footprint. Over the next few days we asked around the neighborhood if anyone had ever heard of an old black man who drove a horse-drawn cart, and eventually found out from a friend's father that years earlier, in the forties and fifties, there was a black man who had a small dairy farm in Tompkins Cove. Every morning he would load up his horse-drawn cart and travel into town to deliver his milk to the local stores. He frequently used the path rather than the main road in order to avoid car traffic. No one had seen him since his farm closed up more than fifteen years earlier, and it was assumed he had moved away or died.

No one else might know what happened to him, but we were sure we knew. He was dead, but at least some nights he still traveled his milk route, pulling his ethereal wares behind him.

Greg Faherty is a published author and certified professional resume writer who owns and operates www.a-perfect-resume. With over fifteen years of experience in technical, scientific, clinical, business, educational, and creative writing, he is a skilled proofreader and editor.

Greg has authored four educational study guides from 2001 to 2004, and contributed large sections of content to more than ten others. Several examples of his short fiction, poetry, and non-fiction have been published through The Princeton Review/McGraw-Hill. He is a member of the Professional Association of Resume Writers and Career Coaches, the Horror Writers of America, and The National Writers Association. He is also the co-author of a monthly advice column, "He Says/She Says," and has recently published in *Chicken Soup for the Teenage Soul*.

Aunt Ruth

by Lori Fauquier

Unfortunately, I was about ten years old when my Aunt Ruth died in a car accident. Words can never describe how I or anyone else in our family grieved. She was someone who touched the lives of many and was taken away from all that loved her. My memories of her still remain in a corner of my heart and I can still see the smile on her face. I miss her dearly even though her love continues to touch me.

Right after her death I was obsessed with Aunt Ruth. Every night before I closed my eyes I would look up at the dark, empty ceiling, asking the questions that no one seemed to be able to answer: Where did she go? Is she OK? Is she happy?

I can't tell you how many nights I did this ritual until my questions were answered. That was a night I will never forget. As usual, I went to bed and asked my questions, wondering if tonight would be the night I would get my answers. As I stared into the ceiling my eyelids became heavy and slowly I drifted off into a state that was somewhere between awake and asleep. This is when I felt someone come into my room. At first I had that scary feeling inside of me—the one you get when you know you have to get up immediately so "they" can't get you but time only seems to go in slow motion. You keep telling yourself—"Wake up! Get up, Lori!" but it doesn't seem to work.

It was then that I felt a person sit at the foot of my bed and put a hand on my leg. At that instant my eyes opened, and there she was—Aunt Ruth with her never-ending smile. "Honey, you don't need to worry about me. I'm all right and I'm very happy. Stop worrying about me," she said. It seemed to last a lifetime that she was sitting there, looking at me and smiling, but with one quick moment she faded into the shadows of the night.

I never told anyone she came to me that night—I kept it to myself. It was a secret that would hold Aunt Ruth and me together even though she was physically gone. I knew from that moment that I did not have to worry about her anymore, and I never asked those questions again.

It wasn't until twenty years later that I would break the secret and tell my mom about that night. I had to break the silence because Aunt Ruth came again in the middle of the night and I didn't know what to do with the vision or experiences I was having.

I had just gone through a divorce to end an abusive relationship when I decided I needed to get away from everything that reminded me of my life. I lost myself and couldn't take the questions anymore from friends and family: "Are you OK?" "It's such a shame you broke up—what happened?" "You know they say you should not date for a year?" and the list goes on and on. I was so desperate to get away that I packed my bags and moved about a thousand miles away to a place where I had no home, no job, and didn't really know anyone.

At first, it was very difficult. I was emotionally a mess, insecure, depressed, with low self-esteem, but I knew I had to do it. Every day I found myself going down to the beach, staring out into the water, and wondering how I got to this place in my life. I read self-help books that never seemed to help and cried every night as I looked up at a dark, empty ceiling asking someone out there to help me because I did not know what to do.

I had completely lost my own identity and I didn't know how to get back. It was then that Aunt Ruth came back into my life.

She came to me the same way she did when I was ten years old. In the middle of the night, she came and sat on my bed and told me not to be afraid or worry about anything, she was here to help me. From that night on things started to change. I'm not even sure if words can describe how I felt or what happened to my life.

All I can say is that slowly I got back everything I had lost in my marriage. I didn't see her again during the night but from time to time I felt this very cold feeling on my right side and I would just say to myself, "Aunt Ruth is that you?" and I would hear a little "Yes" inside my ear as she pushed me along in the right direction.

Don't get me wrong: When she came to me that night and then everything started happening, I was really freaked out, and it scared me. I remembered her coming to me so long ago after her death and now she was coming to me again. I felt I had to tell someone. Could this really be happening? Could she really be helping me? So I did what any girl would do—I called my mom. This is when my mom told me things about my Aunt Ruth, and I realized our connection with her was a lot stronger than I ever imagined.

When Aunt Ruth was alive, she had the ability to know when something was going to happen or when something was wrong. Even though she lived far away from us she always knew when there was a broken heart in our home. We had a connection with her that only words could verify. She would call whenever she could sense there were problems, sadness, or something that needed attention. The only words my mother would hear on the other end of the phone were "Honey, you are having a bad day— tell me about it."

It is from my experiences and the stories my mother told me that I feel that to this day we still have a connection with her. I firmly believe Aunt Ruth's chosen path in the afterworld is to look after her loved ones. I'm not the only one she looks after, but I do know that all I have to do is call her name when I need help. Every day I look at her picture, and as I look into her eyes I know she is literally looking back at me.

Lori Fauquier was born in 1971 in Edison, New Jersey. Writing has always been a deep passion for Lori and she is often inspired by personal life events. She holds a master degree in nursing from Seton Hall University and is currently working as a nurse practitioner. You can reach Lori at lfauquier@yahoo.com.

A Brief Detour

by Rowan Lefwyn

There was never a time I did not believe in a substantial afterlife, a true home we return to after we leave this temporary existence. While ghosts—entities trapped between this world and the next—don't concern me much, spirits—the animated energy of those who have moved on—have made themselves known to me countless times. In spite of this belief, as a young girl I had the same fears of spooks and ghosts and weird noises in the night—until my father's death.

I was only seventeen when my father passed away. I remember clearly every moment of that night twenty-one years ago, an evening so horribly traumatic for a young girl deeply attached to her daddy. Yet this awful time also held the blossoming of a profound yet simple realization: Love transcends all boundaries, and death is not a barrier but simply a door we step through when our time and toil in life here is through.

Spring, 1983. My mother was downstate, visiting relatives, leaving me and Dad to fend for ourselves on our farm in rural Michigan. I had been recovering from a bad case of bronchitis and a toss from a fractious horse. Not badly damaged—just feeling lazy and a bit sorry for myself. So when my dad asked if I wanted to take a late afternoon drive into town, I declined and comfortably settled in for the evening on the couch in front of the tube.

Dad called for our Scottish terrier, Paddy, to accompany him on his excursion. The stout little black dog was always delighted to be invited on a car ride and rushed for the door at the sound of Dad's truck keys. Not long after, I heard my Dad back out the driveway.

I jumped from the couch and looked out the window to make sure Dad was gone. He'd left an unopened pack of cigarettes on the table. Unable to resist (I'd been sneaking the occasional smoke for about a year then), I eased the foil back and took one. Lighting up with the air of a true bon vivant I chatted on the phone with friends, did some homework, and watched one rerun after another.

Then I began to fret a little. Surely Dad would notice the illicit cigarette I'd snuck from his pack. I glanced at the clock and a more immediate worry set in. It was growing late, after ten o'clock, and the realization that I was by myself made me uneasy. We lived in the backwaters; neighbors were few and far between. There weren't even any streetlights. Except for the feeble yellow glow of the sodium lamp over the doorway, there was just utter dark of empty farmland and forests.

Beyond that, I just plain didn't like being in our old house by myself. Built in the 1800s, the floorboards creaked and moaned, and the slightest breeze rattled the windows in their sills. While we never encountered a spook there, our farmhouse seemed an ideal spot for a haunting: old wallpaper, faded and peeling; gloom-shrouded attic; dank earth cellar. If not a haven for any self-respecting ghost, it was fertile ground for a young lady's active imagination. I flinched at every sound, certain someone skulked about the house lying in wait.

Nor was it like Dad to leave me alone for so long, but on the other hand, it was entirely possible he'd run across friends in town. My dad was a congenial, hearty man who counted everyone who crossed his path a friend. Folks loved him as well, for he was quick to buy a drink, had glib wit, and told adventuresome tales of his time in the Navy. So it wouldn't be unusual if he'd been whisked away for a nightcap or a late dinner. He'd simply lost track of time; surely he'd call soon. Whenever Dad was late, he always called to check on me.

I had school the next morning and couldn't wait up. I went to bed, only to toss and turn, growing more anxious with each sleepless moment that passed. Not so much about being in the house by myself or because of the forbidden stolen cigarette, but for my dad. This was long before cell phones were common and there was no way I could even begin to track him down. Why hadn't he called to check on me?

Right about then I heard the crunch of tires on gravel. He was home! I leapt from my bed and listened near my door until I could hear his step on the stairs into the kitchen. I jumped back into bed and pulled the covers to my chin. The kitchen door opened and then shut and I heard his soft step across the dining room to my bedroom door.

"Row?" he said softly. "You all right?"

Feigning sleep, I didn't answer. Now I was annoyed with him for worrying me so and for leaving me alone in our creepy house. Plus I was still a little concerned about that stolen cigarette and didn't want to attract undue attention to myself. I only cracked my eye open a slit, just enough to see his silhouette in the doorway. When I made no reply, he walked away, the dining room floorboards creaking under his weight. When I heard the drop of his boots in his and Mom's bedroom, I felt better. That was a familiar sound, an everyday sound, one that ended each evening —the thud of Dad's heavy boots hitting the floor before he took to his bed.

Reassured, I dozed off.

Only to be awaken not long after by a dreadful banging on the kitchen door. I sat up in bed and glanced at my clock on the nightstand: 11:33 p.m. I tensed, listening for Dad, but I didn't hear him leave the bed. The hard rapping knock came again, and still Dad did nothing.

I rose and hurried to Dad's bedroom. The room was empty, filled only with night-shadow and the big four-poster bed was neatly made—unslept in. Confused, I went to the door and peeked through its window. There was a state trooper standing on the stoop, little Paddy-dog in his arms.

For more than the obvious reasons, I was in disbelief when the trooper regretfully told me that my father had died in a car wreck, just an hour before. "He couldn't have," I began and then trailed off. How could Dad be dead? I heard his truck in the drive, his step in the house, his quiet voice, and most of all, the thump of his boots before he took to his bed.

But for little Paddy-dog wiggling and growling in the trooper's arms I would have denied the horrible truth and slammed the door in the cop's face, unable to bear his pity. Instead, I took Paddy from him and stroked the terrier—Dad's special pet—as he shivered in my arms. Oddly enough, that little dog survived the rollover accident when his master did not.

The trooper called some neighbors to sit with me while I made one phone call after another. Determined to be brave I did not cry, but dialed number after number in a kind of numb suspension, removed from it all. The whole time I thought, Dad can't be dead. He'll come home.

Then it struck me; he had come to me. One last time, Dad had came to check on his little girl who was still scared of the dark and things that went bump in the night. Dad had made a brief detour to his earthly home before moving on to his eternal one, to make sure I was all right.

Politely I asked the neighbors to leave—I wanted to be by myself to think this out. They were unwilling, but I was adamant.

After they had left, I sat at the dining room table to wait for the sun's rise that would bring my devastated mother and grieving family.

I felt grief-stricken and yet calm, filled with the illuminating realization that he'd come to me before going on.

Then I found the dark of night and its shadows of death didn't frighten me quite so much anymore.

————————

Rowan Lefwyn is a speculative fiction writer who recently completed her third novel. Rowan's experiences with the paranormal have led her to explore otherworldly events through fiction and non-fiction. Her interests vary from equestrian sports to ale making to Celtic wisdom, and she particularly loves a good ghost story. Rowan's otherwise idle hours are spent as a cell leader for the novel writers forum Z-7 Speculative Fiction, and as an editor for Atsoise e-zine. You can visit Rowan at www.RowanLefwyn.com/RowanLefwyn.html and at www.soul-engravings.com.

A Grandmother's Story

by Linda L. Porter

My family lived with great-grandma St. John until she passed away when I was nine years old. After her first stroke Grandma was partially paralyzed on one side. The doctors told her she would never walk again, but she was stubborn and proved them wrong. Even so, she still experienced some paralysis and she couldn't manage to get her right foot totally off the floor. As her slipper scuffed across the hardwood floor it made a distinct sound. This made it easier for my sister and me to stay out of trouble, as we always knew when she was coming.

It was two weeks after the funeral when we heard her walking around in her room for the first time. I was frightened and tried to pretend that I didn't hear; besides I was sure everyone would think I was crazy. I looked at my mom; she was reading and didn't seem to hear anything. Then I glanced at my father. The look on his face told me I wasn't the only one who heard it. Not saying a word, my father stood up and headed toward Grandma's room. Wanting to know if it actually was Grandma coming back to visit, I followed close behind. As Dad reached for the doorknob, the noise suddenly stopped. When he opened the door, there was nothing there. All that lingered was the fragrance of lilacs, her favorite flower.

That was the first encounter we experienced with our ghostly grandmother. After that, little things started to happen.

Her favorite black sweater appeared on the back of the chair where she always kept it. A few days later my mother found Grandma's favorite pin sitting on her dresser. Grandma loved that pin and never left the house without it. It was the last gift Grandpa gave her before he passed away. The pin, along with most of her things, had been packed away in the closet after she died.

Grandma always drank black tea; she believed people lived longer if they drank tea every day. While cleaning out the cupboard one afternoon my mother ran across the box of tea. No one else in the family drank tea so she threw it in the trash. It really freaked her out when she found the box of tea back on the cupboard shelf the next morning. She grabbed it and threw it into the trash again. This happened several times over the next couple of weeks until Mom insisted my father take the tea to work and pitch it. The tea never showed up in the cupboard again. Sometimes when we entered Grandma's room, her rocking chair would be rocking back and forth with no one in it. The scent of lilacs always accompanied each incident. At first my parents thought my sister and I were moving the items—until the tea episode: We were vacationing at my aunt's farm at the time.

Little things kept happening over a period of several months. Never once were we afraid nor did we feel threatened in any way. That is until the Friday night my sister and I will never forget. We were lying in bed whispering back and forth. My mother had already yelled up the stairs for us to get to sleep so were trying to be quiet. Suddenly we heard Grandma's unmistakable walk. We knew it was Grandma because her slipper was scuffing the floor as it always did. It sounded as if she were climbing the stairs, which was ridiculous as Grandma had not been able to use the stairs for several months before she died. We stopped talking and listened, all the while keeping an eye on the bedroom door but nothing happened. The sound of her walk ended just as quickly as it started.

Thinking nothing more was going to happen, we snuggled down in bed to sleep. Unexpectedly I saw movement out of the corner of my eye. I glanced at the door and there she was. Grandma St. John stood at the top of the stairs right outside of our bedroom door. She was smiling at us. I don't know how long I stared at her before turning to my sister. All the color had drained from her face and her eyes were wide open. We watched as Grandma held out her arms as if to hold us. Her mouth was moving but no words came out. Suddenly my sister blurted out, "I think she is saying 'I love you.'"

We watched for a couple of minutes, then decided we would go to her, wanting to feel Grandma's comforting arms around us again. Neither wanted to be the first to approach her so we each tried to get the other to climb out of bed and go to her. It took me several minutes to finally muster up enough nerve to rise out of bed. I just stood there staring at her, not sure if I really wanted to go any closer. I was shaking as I slowly walked toward Grandma. As I approached her, I felt an overwhelming sense of peace and comfort. I wanted to touch her more than anything, yet was still uneasy. After all, she was dead and I had never seen a ghost before.

I inched closer, one little step at a time, talking to her as I went. When I was only a couple of feet away I stopped. She reached up and motioned me to come closer. I took a couple more steps and reached out to touch her hand. As my hand was about to touch hers she seemed to move farther away. I didn't actually see her move, yet no matter how close I got it seemed she was always a couple of inches out of my reach. When I stopped to ponder my next move, she slowly disappeared. Not vanishing suddenly, but gradually fading away. When she was barely visible, my sister and I both started calling for my father, but by the time he reached the top of the stairs Grandma was nowhere to be seen. The only thing that alluded to her presence was the lingering fragrance of lilacs.

We never saw Grandma's ghost or heard her walking after that night. I feel her final appearance was her way of telling us "I love you and I am now at peace." She had said her good-byes and there was no need for her to linger on. Every spring when the lilacs are in bloom and their fragrance fills the air I smile and think of Grandma St. John.

Linda Porter is a writer, poet, and miniaturist. The mother of three boys—Frank, Patrick, and Christopher—she resides in Portage, Michigan. She has written more than 150 poems, several short stories, and is currently working on a children's picture book. She has also published several poems including "The Greatest Love," "He is There," and "Tunnel of Darkness."

All in the Family

by Diane Steinbach

I grew up in a psychic family. Grandma had the gift, Mom had it, Sis has it, and I have it. We live with it as if it were as natural as green eyes and brown hair. We always believed it was just part of normal existence to get messages from the beyond, to know when someone close to you is in trouble, and to ask and receive help from the other side.

As I got into my late twenties, I learned more about tapping into those natural gifts, and my spiritual encounters escalated. I learned how to contact my spirit guides and how to ask for ways to help the other people in this world. Apparently I had opened a door in my mind that is often passed by, and a whole new realm of experiences awaited.

It began slowly. I tried my hand at giving "readings" and found that the spirit guides around me were helping the people I touched with information about lost family members and personal health issues, and with guidance for their life journeys. Overall, the experiences were positive, but sometimes the information I was getting was troubling. Sometimes I was unsure, reluctant, about passing on information I received. Even though a question might have been asked about a spouse's fidelity or a grandparent's life expectancy, I wondered whether the person really wanted to know.

Often I would get messages for people I barely knew. How would they receive it? Would they think I was crazy? Once the grandmother of a store clerk I was familiar with only in passing wanted me to march right back into the store and tell him she was there! I refused, fearing I would be labeled a crazy lady, so she sat in my car and rode a few blocks toward my home with me. That time I won the argument, but I didn't always.

I fought the spirit world sometimes, but they finally convinced me that when it came to certain things, I had given up my right to make those choices. For example, I shared an office with a friend named Terri (not her real name). I had gotten to know her fairly well in the four or five years we worked together. I knew she was very religious; she knew I was psychic. Sometimes we would talk about her skepticism regarding psychic phenomenon. Eventually we just stopped talking about it altogether. We had a high regard for each other's honesty, integrity, and beliefs, and found it better not to argue over issues that seemed could not be proven or disproved.

One day I arrived at the office to find out that Terri had rushed off to the hospital in a nearby town. Her mother had been in a terrible car accident and they didn't give her long to live. The town was two hours away. Although they drove at breakneck speeds, Terri and her husband arrived too late. Devastated, Terri longed for a final good-bye and would never receive it. So she thought.

I felt bad for Terri. I hadn't met her mother, but I knew they shared a strong bond and that the loss would be painful and lifelong. Terri's parents had divorced when she was quite young, and because she didn't know much about her father, her mother was her only parental connection.

That night I went to bed thinking of my friend. I wondered what I could do or say to help her get through this terrible time. I lay awake in the dimly lit room. I asked my spirit guides to help me come up with the right words, the right actions to make the pain a little less for my friend. I began to doze off but just as my eyes were about to close, I felt a presence. My eyes blinked open wide to see the darkened silhouette of a woman beside my bed. Although I had never seen her, I knew it was Terri's mom. I could make out the shape of her hair, her size. I had an idea of what she was wearing and could see the wringing of her hands. She stood next to me, close enough to touch me, but there was no touch. She communicated nothing, and my initial fear and surprise at her presence prompted me to ask my spirits to remove her. She disappeared and I suffered a restless night's sleep.

The next night she appeared to me again. This time she told me I needed to tell Terri she was all right. I was supposed to tell her daughter that she need not worry about her any longer. I understood, but I resisted. I didn't want to upset Terri with what I feared she would interpret as psychic babble from a well-meaning friend.

Each day I resisted became harder than the last. Terri's mother was persistent. I tried to communicate to her my uncertainty and that I was afraid to talk to Terri. Her mother showed her displeasure at my reluctance by creating illusions of my home in chaos. Although she never actually became destructive, she kept me awake for three days with images of flying televisions, unexplained noises, and swirling photos and knickknacks. It was a haunting. She was displeased, and she wasn't taking "no" for an answer.

I felt beaten, and finally made an opportunity to talk to Terri about her mother. I took her aside and explained that her mother had visited me, and that she wanted—needed—Terri to know she was all right. She needed to tell her that she had made it, and that she knew Terri had come to the hospital that fateful day.

Terri started crying. Immediately I was unsure if I had done the right thing. I didn't want to upset her, but I had to do as her mother had asked. Terri finally looked up at me and said, " Thank God, Diane. I have been asking her in my prayers to find a way to let me know she was all right! I have been praying for an answer, and she came to you to let me know!" We hugged and I felt the presence of Terri's mother around us. I told her so.

Since this event I have communicated with many people's loved ones on the other side. Sometimes they have answers for long-wondered questions, sometimes they just want to say "Hi" and "I am here!" All the messages are important, and I have learned that I am just an instrument of communication to bridge this world with the next. It's part of my genetics, my family history; it's who I am.

Diane Steinbach is an art therapist, writer, and columnist. Her books *The Practical Guide to Art Therapy Groups* (Fausek: Haworth Press Inc., 1997) and *Art Activities for Groups: Providing Therapy, Fun, and Function* (Idyll Arbor Inc., 2002) are available at Amazon.com. Her third book, *Art as Therapy: Inspiration, Innovation and Ideas*, was released in November 2004.

The Whispered Kiss

by Erin Kastner

Bill was the first friend I made at my new summer job building office furniture, a vocation uncommon for a female. As my boss, he showed me the ropes—always with a smile on his face and thumbs hooked through his jeans belt loops. He never criticized and was quick to cheer me up with a joke when I was upset after making a mistake. I'm sure Bill was the reason I stuck it out, lugging sheets of plywood and tending blisters from using the drill.

He walked around the shop, dragging his feet as if his boots were too big, always with laces coming undone. It was an endearing quality I came to notice and enjoy. He was one of those nice, genuine guys that women seem to avoid for silly reasons like "he's not enough of a bad boy."

He quickly introduced me to his friends and we all spent time together, usually going to dance clubs on weekends. Bill never failed to make sure he had more fun than most, acting more like a thirteen-year-old rather than a thirty-year-old. Over the years his friends became as much mine as his, and eventually a love triangle came to light. I had never thought of Bill that way—he was first my boss and then my friend. But when the opportunity made itself clear I found myself thinking long and hard about whether to choose him or our mutual friend Dave. Dave was definitely of the "bad boy" variety—driving a sports car, wearing cowboy boots with jeans and a black leather jacket in the middle of the summer. He was the kind of guy who would wear sunglasses even if it were raining. Bill was Bill, dragging his loosely tied boots and cracking jokes. I chose the bad boy, but in my defense I was young and worried about the seven-year age difference between Bill and me.

For nine months I dated Dave, but things became strained and soon after we broke up I noticed him flirting with a friend of mine. There were no hard feelings though; I knew already that bad boy wasn't meant for me. Dave ended up marrying my friend but they later divorced. Through it all, Bill remained the good friend he'd become. He'd call me up and urge me to come out dancing, and I always loved his company. My thoughts again turned to him with a tinge of regret that I hadn't chosen him over Dave. Maybe Bill and I would have had a better go of it, but it was too late to find out. Dave and Bill were still close friends and it didn't seem right. I also considered how lucky I was that Dave and I were still amiable and I hadn't been alienated from the wonderful friends I'd made in their crowd. If Bill and I had dated and it hadn't worked out, I anticipated two outcomes. One, it might not be so amiable and I would be badly hurt by losing a good friend and two, I wouldn't be able to face our circle of friends again.

Over time I moved to a different suburb of our city and made other friends. Occasionally both crowds would come together but more and more I found myself spending time with the new crowd. One night I took one of my new friends to my old favorite hangout where I used to spend time with Bill and the others. Much to my delight, they were there! It was like a reunion of sorts, but at the same time they welcomed me like they'd just seen me yesterday. It seemed strange that they didn't seem to greet me with the same elation I felt at seeing them. They seemed quiet and subdued, not their usual energetic selves. One person was missing from the crowd, and after Larry took his shot at the six ball and stepped away from the pool table, I asked him where Bill was. His blunt response, I later understood, was his way of coping with the news he had just heard himself. Bill had died. At home, in his sleep, and alone.

The next twenty-four hours were a blur for me, almost surreal. I remember my friend getting me back to her house and I remember sitting on the floor of her bedroom, crying my eyes out and waking her parents. I remember driving home in the rain the next day to find my sister and her family with Dave, sitting at the dining room table, grieving.

I found myself surprised at how hard the loss had hit me. I had only experienced the death of a loved one once before, but it was nothing like this. My grandmother, by all admissions, not just my own, was a hard woman to love and I'd always been more afraid of her than loved her.

With Bill it was different. I realized how much I had loved him and appreciated him, and now the love was lost for good. The feeling of regret for not choosing him was now permanent. To this day my only regret in life is that I didn't explore the possibility that Bill could have been the love of my life. After finally hugging my family and Dave goodnight, the feeling of regret and loss were so intense I could not sleep even though I was exhausted from the grieving.

I tried to reason with myself that I needed sleep, since I hadn't had any the night before, sitting on the floor of my friend's bedroom. I told myself I had to stop thinking, stop feeling, and just rest, that tomorrow would be another hard day. I had no discipline though, and my thoughts kept coming back to Bill. Just when I thought I had no more tears left, they would come.

Then, when I was at my very lowest, gasping for breath with tears streaming down my face and onto my already-soaked pillow, I heard a voice. Actually a whisper, and a very distinct whisper at that, directly into my left ear. That whisper was one word—"kiss." I immediately stopped crying and went rigid with fear. The whisper was so close to my ear I could almost feel it. The room was dark and the door was closed—just as I had left it—so someone must have come into my room before me and hid. As soon as that thought came into my head I dismissed it and an immense feeling of peace came over me. Physically, I was alone. The fear and sorrow left me and I understood with perfect clarity. Bill had kissed me—I knew this with as much certainty as I knew my name. Without even thinking about it, I also understood that logically, Bill was in spirit form now and without a body he could not have physically kissed me. That was the reason for the whisper. It was just like him, to try to cheer me up. There was no regret or loss anymore because I understood Bill was with me—still and forever.

Although I was raised to believe there is life after death, until that night I didn't truly believe. Since that night I have never felt such an overwhelming amount of grief when I've lost a loved one. I understand they are truly with me in spirit, that we are closer than ever, and that gives me peace. When I visit Bill's grave I thank him for his eternal gift of that knowledge and comfort and I always say "kiss" before I leave.

Erin Kastner has been writing since the age of thirteen when she began writing poetry. It became clear very quickly though that short stories and essays were her passion. She began writing seriously after winning an honorable mention in a province-wide essay writing competition on the subject of "imagination." Her other passion is sustainable living and in recent years most of her writing has focused on "treading lightly." She believes her spirituality makes her more open to the acceptance of the supernatural, and all aspects of existence bring her much joy and inspiration.

Gram Foster's House

by Jensen Foster

"Thank you so much for consenting to such an unusual request," I said to the real estate agent, Deborah, as she unlocked the door to the house and ushered me inside.

"It's my pleasure, Ms. Foster. This house has been on the market for quite some time. According to my papers," she began flipping through a folder she held in her hands, "Oh, here it is. Yes, this house has been sold a number of times. Three to be exact, in the past thirteen years, and none of the owners have resided here long. It's kind of strange. Wouldn't you say? Almost as if the house is…."

"Haunted?" I responded, before she had time to complete her sentence.

"Well… yes… that was sort of along the lines I was thinking." She gave me a tentative look. Pursing her lips together the agent looked about the entryway nervously and then said, "This is the first time the house has been put up for sale by our company. The present owners moved to Moncton, New Brunswick. He works for Atlantic Wholesalers and was transferred back there six months ago."

My eyes scanned the kitchen and the neat rows of cupboards. Just as I remembered it, minus the big wooden table in the corner and the oven over to the left of the window that faced out onto the backyard. I remembered with amusement that Gram was

140

constantly leaving the stove on and catching her oven mitts and tea towels on fire. My mother used to always say, "She's gone and burned up another pair!" My father lived in fear that she would one day burn down the house around her and perish in a fiery blaze. She did die in this house but it didn't happen that way at all.

"Ms. Foster! Ms. Foster! Are you all right?"

I turned around abruptly at the sound of Deborah's voice.

"I'm sorry," I said as I shook my head to clear it. "What were you saying?"

"Oh, I was just wondering, did you say when you phoned that you had once lived in this house?"

"No," I responded, "not lived, just visited." I walked into the kitchen and stood in the center of the room. I could almost see myself as a child, peeking at the pots on the stove and enjoying the delicious aroma of Gram Foster's cooking.

"My paternal grandmother lived here for many years, at least all the years I knew her. Gram, as us kids used to call her, died in this house in April of 1989."

Deborah gave a shudder and I turned to stare at her, giving her my full attention for the first time since we had entered the house.

"Did I say something wrong?"

"No, no, it's just that…." her voice trailed off. "There is nothing in my files about… ah… the owners of this house that goes that far back but…." Her eyes met mine. "I grew up in these parts, Ms. Foster, and there has been talk from time to time. Not that I believe any of it of course, but still…."

"Talk?" I was a little mystified. "As in this house just might be haunted? Ms…. what did you say your last name was?"

"Brownell, Deborah Brownell. And it's Mrs. not Ms. I grew up right here in this area. Did you visit often when you were growing up, Ms. Foster?"

"Yes, quite often. I loved it here. I used to help Gram out in her garden, and we'd sit out on the verandah on hot summer afternoons and eat strawberry ice cream cones. It was the simple life but I enjoyed it very much. I cherish my memories of that time."

"It sounds like you loved your grandmother very much."

"I did. Very much."

Mrs. Brownell was eager to get off the topic of haunted houses. That was obvious to me.

"The big dining room table was there," I said, motioning to the middle of the dining room, "and Gram's china cabinet was here." I pointed to the right side of the wall, opposite the entry to the rectangular-shaped room. "Her dishes were lovely! White with pink designs, if I recall. And those teacups and saucers—how I loved them! They were so delicate looking and so... well, from a different time, a different place. I...."

"Ms. Foster, I don't mean to hurry you along or anything as I know this house is full of so many memories for you but I really must...."

We both turned our heads abruptly as we heard a thud come from one of the upstairs bedrooms. Neither one of us spoke for a minute, but the real estate agent didn't need to—fear was written all over her face.

"I'm sure it's just a bedroom window that was left open," I said, glancing out the dining room window. "It looks like a breeze has come up. Should I go take a look now or should we both venture upstairs?" I looked at her innocently, already knowing what answer I was going to get.

"No! No!" she exclaimed loudly. She held her hand out to stop me as I made a move to leave the room and investigate the noise. "I'm sure you are right, Ms. Foster. No need to worry. A bedroom window left open sounds like a plausible explanation." She turned and scurried back into the kitchen. I followed after her.

"I'm going to wait out in the car for you, Ms. Foster, give you some privacy. Take your time. Don't hurry on my account. I'm not allowed to leave the premises but the driveway is not leaving the premises, right? Any questions you have for me I'll be happy to answer after you are finished, with your... ah... tour of the house." She was talking so quickly that her words were almost running together. "So, um, I'll see you when you're done, OK?" Clutching her purse to her chest she made a beeline for the door. "Out in the car is where I will be if you need me, but you shouldn't as you know your way around quite well."

"OK," I answered to the sound of the slamming door. Mrs. Brownell seemed to be running down the steps to reach the safety of her car. "This house is not haunted," I uttered to an empty room.

I retraced my steps through the dining room and went into the living room. Slowly and methodically I began my tour around Gram Foster's former residence.

It was time, I realized. I could not avoid it any longer. I had to see for myself, with my own eyes, the area at the foot of the stairs where she was found dead, clutching the telephone receiver in her hand. She knew that she couldn't stop the bleeding and that she needed help desperately in order to save herself but she was too weak and too... too... what? I did not have the answers.

I held my breath as I looked at the empty spot where her desk had once stood at the foot of the stairs. I felt my heart speed up as I imagined my grandmother, terrified at the sight of her bleeding leg, doing what she could to stop the bleeding but to no avail. Then rushing as fast as her phlebitis-ridden legs could carry her, in pain and discomfort, reaching for the phone to call someone, anyone, to help her, but not making it in time. Instead, being overcome by unconsciousness and collapsing into death still grasping the phone in her hand. The knowledge of that had haunted my dreams most of all. It still did. I could not rid the image from my overactive mind.

When I had anticipated this moment, standing here in the spot in the house where she had taken her last, dying breath, I imagined that I would be filled with horror and desperation at what had taken place but instead I felt … freer somehow and less burdened by the problems that plagued my life.

Feeling more courageous than I had when I first arrived, I carefully walked over to the spot where her life had ended. Reaching out for the banister, I made my way up the steep, twisting staircase to the top floor of the house. I had always had a fear of falling and hurting myself on those stairs when I was a little girl. They seemed even more difficult for me to negotiate now that I was an adult woman.

After perusing the three upstairs bedrooms and the bathroom, I decided that it was getting late and I should finish up soon and take my leave. Poor Deborah Brownell was probably shivering in her car and anxious to leave the property at once. Shadows had begun to fall across the back lawn. I did not want to be spooked or to feel fear or apprehension in this house. I had come to make peace with my past in a sense.

Something in the back of my mind would not grant me any rest or allow me to move on. That is why I had come. To let go and to move beyond. Move beyond what exactly, I was not sure.

Watching my steps carefully, I made my way down the stairs and returned to the main floor. I knew it was time to go. My heart felt buoyant and I knew with certainty that I had accomplished at least part of what I had come here to do.

How long had I been in here? I glanced at my watch. It was almost six-thirty. Darkness was beginning to descend and I did not want to be here when the process was complete. I had gotten so caught up in my walk down memory lane that to save my life, I could not remember what time Deborah and I had arrived.

Stopping yet again in the dreaded spot at the foot of the stairs, I looked at the wall opposite the door and remembered something that had slipped my mind earlier. There had once been a mirror there, a very old-looking ornate mirror. I used to think it an unusual spot to put a mirror. I stared at that spot on the wall, conjuring up an image of it in happier days.

Without any warning, I saw the mirror as if it were still hanging there. It was there! I looked into it and saw nothing at first but the wall behind me. I was transfixed by its appearance. An image of a person appeared, first shadowy, as if the person were far away, and then moving closer, into sharper focus. The hair on the back of my neck stood up. I broke out in a sweat. I was terrified of what I was witnessing.

A ghost in the mirror! Oh my God, no… or yes… it was… Gram, yes it was Gram Foster, looking calm and peaceful, wearing her favorite flowery dress. She looked exactly as I remembered her. I couldn't believe it. It was her! It was my Gram!

Startled, my eyes widened and I stumbled backward, narrowly missing hitting my head on the railing of the staircase. My heart threatened to beat out of my chest. I shook my head from side to side to decide whether I was dreaming or wide-awake. I closed my eyes tight.

I was indeed wide-awake I assured myself as I tentatively stole a glance at the spot on the wall where the mirror had suddenly appeared. It was still there, clear as day. I wasn't imagining a thing. This was really happening to me. The entire area I was in had taken on a surreal quality. I stood up on legs that felt like jelly and moved in closer to get a better look.

Yes, there was no denying it. Gram was staring out at me from the mirror. The Gram I remembered so well and had loved so very much. She looked happy, I was pleased to see, so very happy. I was looking at the past and the dearly departed, both in the same instance. But was I looking into the other side of life as well? Was I looking into the face of death?

I stood there, staring into the mirror. I was mesmerized. She smiled at me, ever so slightly. I returned the smile in kind. And then she was gone. As suddenly as she had appeared, her image faded and she simply disappeared.

I blinked my eyes a couple of times but knew in my heart that the mirror would no longer be there. I was correct; it was gone too. It was over with. My mission, whatever it had been, my reason for wanting to visit this house, had been accomplished.

"Ms. Foster! OH, MY GOD!! What's happened to you? You look positively frightful!"

Shocked to hear a voice, I turned to see Deborah Brownell burst through the entryway. I must have looked a sight, as I stood transfixed, staring glassy-eyed into empty space on a wall.

"Oh, oh…." I found myself at a complete loss for words. My heartbeat was only now beginning to return to normal and my legs still felt very unsteady. I sat down on the bottom step of the stairs to gain my bearings.

"Are you OK, Ms. Foster? You look like you've seen…." Deborah didn't finish what she was about to say. I knew what she was alluding to but was not about to tell her the truth.

Hanging my head down, I rubbed my forehead and tried to get hold of the emotions that raced through my head at an alarming rate. What in heaven's name had just happened here?

Once I had my emotions in check I glanced up at Deborah, who sported a frightened look. Taking a deep breath and then letting it out slowly I said, "I'm ready to go."

I stood up. I really was ready to leave. A sense of calm was coming over me and I knew that I had set, whatever needed to be set, right. Things were now as they were supposed to be.

"But you're so white, Ms. Foster, even your lips are drained of color. Perhaps you should...."

I held up my hand. "Thank you for your concern but really it's not necessary. I am fine, more than fine actually. I'm ready to leave. I have seen all I need to see." I began to make my way down the hallway and back to the front entrance.

Following behind me I heard Deborah utter in a less than convincing manner, "Well… OK… if you're certain you are all right and sure that you've seen everything you need to."

"I have."

I reached the front door and turned back to take a look at the interior of Gram's house. I was glad I had come back for one final time. It was well worth the trip.

Deborah said nothing as she locked the house and made her way over to her car. Her silence continued as she opened her door.

I stood looking at the yard and the grounds before holding out my hand to the real estate agent.

"Thank you, Mrs. Brownell, for taking the time to bring me out here to see the house. I know it took time away from your work, but I do appreciate the opportunity to come here again and look around one last time."

Smiling, she responded warmly, "It was my pleasure, Ms. Foster, and please, call me Deborah."

"OK, Deborah, thank you. And you can call me Jensen."

"Jensen it is."

I made a move to walk over to my car but Deborah stopped me with a hand on my shoulder. Curious, I faced her. She had a very serious, solemn look on her face.

"Jensen, if you don't mind me asking… I know it's none of my business… I'm only the real estate agent but did you get what you came for? Here at the house, I mean? Today?"

I stared at her, almost through her, as my mind wandered back to the afternoon I had spent in the house, ending with the bizarre experience with the nonexistent mirror.

"I sensed a need for closure or something close to it on your part when we arrived this afternoon. And the look on your face when I walked in…."

Looking at the house, all the way up to the roof and the chimney and then back again, I smiled in a dreamlike fashion and said in a voice that sounded far away to my own ears, "Yes. Yes. I got what I came for. Nothing more, nothing less." I sounded more as though I were talking to myself than to someone else.

"Good," Deborah said, sounding a little miffed, "I'm glad then, Jensen. It was not a wasted afternoon for either of us then."

"Definitely not wasted," I answered. "Do you think you will sell the house?" I asked before once again moving in the direction of my car.

"I'm certainly going to try." Deborah smiled, and I knew she meant it. "It was nice meeting you, Jensen. Perhaps I will bump into you again some time. And if you're ever interested in property, you know who to call. Take care of yourself."

"You too, Deborah. And I'll keep that in mind." I smiled back at her. As I placed my key in the lock, a thought occurred to me. I called over to Deborah, "This house is not haunted, Deborah. You have nothing to fear. It is full of only goodness and love."

"What?" I saw Deborah cup her ear and mouth the word as she backed her car out of the driveway.

I repeated myself, even louder this time, but to no avail. She couldn't hear me over the sound of her engine. Or maybe she didn't even want to. A quick getaway was still lying heavily on her mind. How could I blame her? It had been an intense afternoon for both of us.

I watched Deborah's car disappear down the road, in the opposite direction from where I was headed. Putting my car in reverse, I edged my way out of the long driveway. Just as I put the car into gear something caught my eye.

The house stood with the shadows of night creeping over it like a thick fog. A light had come on upstairs. I knew that I had not left any of them on. It was the light in the bedroom facing the front of the house, directly above where her favorite flowers, petunias, used to grow. Gram's room.

Feeling a shiver up my spine, I smiled knowingly. Everything did not need an explanation. Some things were better left alone.

With that I took off down the road, away from the house.

It was the last time for me. I drove away from Gram Foster's house and all that remained inside. The past was gone, it was over with, but I had been left with so much. I could move on with my life now. I had come for insight and closure and I had found both.

Good-bye, Gram Foster. Good-bye to your house in the valley. Thank you, from your granddaughter Jensen. Thank you from the bottom of my heart. I Love You. Good-bye.

Jensen Foster is a freelance writer from Canada who wonders if another "haunted encounter" is in her future. She almost hopes so! Ever since she was a young girl she has had a fascination with "the other side," as she refers to it. Besides writing about her own experiences, Jensen also writes on a variety of topics including gardening and pets. She is currently collaborating on a book about pirates and buried treasure with another author. Jensen is a voracious reader, practices yoga and meditation on a regular basis, and enjoys playing tennis. Jensen lives with her husband, Jase, their daughter, Madison Lynn, and three cats in Nova Scotia, Canada.

Sign of the Feather

by Carolyn Marie Frassa

The nuns told us that if we were good we would go to heaven, to an afterlife, a place where it was beautiful, and we could do whatever we wanted. I doubted that many times as I was growing up. How did the nuns know what happens to us after we were gone? Certainly no one ever came back to tell us. At least that's what I thought.

My dearly loved mother passed away eighteen days after being diagnosed with cancer that had spread undetected throughout her entire body. We were numb with grief and remorse over not noticing the subtle signs that would have sent us for medical help sooner. Now I wanted so hard to believe that she lived on in that eternal paradise; that she was happy and free of pain; and that she could see us and know that we missed her and loved her still. Not two months went by when her sister also passed away. It was a rough time.

My mother was a gentle woman who besides loving her family deeply also loved animals and birds. We had a steady stream of strays under our roof. My father would always say no more animals, but more always followed. Once when we were kids, my mother saw a squirrel in the yard eating some bread she had put out for the birds. She ran to get my father's 8mm movie camera and filmed the squirrel. My father had all the old movie film transferred to videotape several years ago, and once in a while I put those tapes on and see that long-forgotten squirrel or some ducks at a nearby pond that she filmed.

She was forever putting food out for the birds and had several birdhouses and a birdbath in her yard. She would sit on her porch and watch them. She was amazed with their gift of flight and said on many occasions, "I wish I could fly like a bird." Of course, after they finished eating they would fly over my father's car in the driveway. My father loves his cars as much as she loved the birds. The rumor is that the owner of the local car wash put three kids through college on my father's frequent visits. Subtle hints were dropped, but my mother always said they were God's creatures too. My father didn't argue with her.

Anyway, I had this nagging feeling for the longest time that if I could just talk to her one more time, or just know that she did live on, I would be able to accept what happened.

My sister arranged for us to see Jim, a man who she had been told could communicate with the dead. I went out of curiosity and the overwhelming urge to talk to my mother once again. I wasn't disappointed with the meeting, but it hadn't been an earth-shattering experience. He met with me for close to an hour. He was a very spiritual man who strongly believed that our life does not end after our time on earth. He told me that my mother communicated to him that she was all right and was with members of her family that had predeceased her and also with her sister who had passed over shortly after she did.

He told me I have to keep my eyes open. He said that I would see a balloon or a feather floating in the breeze and that would be a sign from her that she was there and that she was OK.

A couple of months passed and the weather became warm again. It was one of those beautiful spring days when it seems all the birds that had flown south for the winter had just arrived back in town, a day my mother would have spent sitting on her porch after filling all her bird feeders to the brim.

I was on the deck on the side of my house barbecuing our dinner when I heard the loudest chirping coming from the tree at the end of my driveway about twenty-five feet away. I looked over and saw two red cardinals sitting on a branch about halfway up the tree. They were both facing me and still chirping louder now as if they wanted to hold my attention. I said to my children, "There's my mother and her sister." I said it as a joke, but I always thought that if my mother could have had a wish upon her arrival in heaven, it would have been to spend some time "to fly like a bird."

I stood and stared for a moment at those two birds, realizing what I had just said. I soon went back to my dinner cooking on the grill until the noise from those two beautiful birds grew to such a pitch, I had to stop again and stand at the fence that separated the backyard from the front. It was as if they were trying to tell me something. After a couple minutes more of their lively conversation, they turned their heads and took flight.

I watched them for as long as I could until they became two specks in the sky. I stepped back from the fence I was leaning on and was about to turn when I saw a big red feather floating in the air. It looked like that feather from *Forrest Gump*. I watched it float ever so slowly toward the ground and head in my direction. I was frozen in place as I watched this feather that had started its descent about thirty feet from me float closer and closer to where I was standing.

As it neared the fence, I was tempted to stretch way over to grab it in midair, but I didn't. I stood firmly in my spot and it was now inches from the ground. I thought it would land on the other side of the fence. Without even the slightest wisp of a breeze, the red feather hugged the ground and floated under the wooden fence. It came to rest on my foot and didn't move until I bent down and picked it up.

I stared at the feather in my hand, not really looking at it, but processing the thoughts that were now going through my head. My thoughts raced back to the meeting I had had with Jim. Suddenly I just knew. I called to my children, who hadn't been too interested after I first pointed out the two birds. I opened my hand to show them the feather. They seemed puzzled about why their mother was so interested in those two birds and a feather. I realized that I could never explain this to them without them thinking I had totally lost it, so I took the feather and put it in my pocket.

Later that evening I took the feather and put it in a trinket box that I keep on my night table beside the bed. I know now that we do live on. I have the feather to prove it!

Carolyn Frassa was born in Brooklyn, New York. She is the oldest of three children and has lived on Long Island for most of her life. Carolyn is the mother of two children, a son and a daughter. Her son is a sophomore in college who is striving to become a social worker. Her daughter recently completed her master's degree and began teaching English at a school in Manhattan.

Carolyn is in the information technology field, but her first love has always been writing. She has been a freelance writer for many years and has published several human-interest stories and occasional political op-ed pieces. Her drive for politics and interest in spirituality has been her main motivation and inspiration when writing. Her writing style is reminiscent of Garrison Keillor but always holds Carolyn's own twist and punch, allowing it to be exciting, sentimental, thoughtful, and thought-provoking.

Carolyn has a love of books and nature, and is an avid reader and gardener. She sees writing as one would use a camera. She hunts for moments to capture but rather than through a photograph she captures them through her words.

Grandmother's Wisdom

by Denise Broussard

The wisdom of our ancestors goes beyond the grave, for they hold infinite knowledge. And sometimes, if we listen, they will bring it to us, guiding us to safety.

My maternal grandmother was a beautiful, elegant woman. She always dressed for any occasion, from country club brunches to simple garden work. Such highly visible traits were more than evident. However, less obvious, until her death in 1985, was the fact that she'd held me in high esteem.

In the mid-1990s, Grandmother swept into my dreams. Every year, around the time of her birth and death, she made her nocturnal visits. In these dreams, I always sat upright in bed, turning to watch my sleeping self. Grandmother always appeared as if she were in her early thirties. She stood only a few feet from my side. Her hair was perfectly styled as if she'd just stepped out of the beauty salon. Each time she wore the same pale blue dress with a matching belt. Hanging from the crook of her right arm was a wicker handbag. She had the most beautiful face, as if it were light molded into her shape. Glorious blue eyes sparkled at me. And she always smiled but never spoke.

Until 1999. The other odd thing was that she appeared when I was in trouble. I was struggling to free myself from a torturous relationship and had recently found a place to move.

When Grandmother appeared, her frown went from her lips, following the contours of her eyes and into the tiny crevices of worry lines on her forehead. "Child, listen to me," urgency reigning in the tone, "you must get away. He's going to hurt you. He's going to pull a knife on you." Grandmother held up a hunting knife, the slick blade at least six inches long. "Get away, child, before he kills you." She faded away, her words still echoing in my mind as I woke.

Sweat soaked my clothes. Icy chills made me shiver. I didn't know what to think but I knew, inevitably, what I would do.

My ex terrified me, and through that fear, even though I was warned, I allowed him to manipulate me into showing him where I was to move.

The small trailer was located at the edge of a valley, sheltered beneath a grove of junipers. The spot was far from town and isolated. I did not have a telephone. What was I thinking, showing that man my home? Terror had its hold on me and I could not escape.

One night, long after the moon had risen above the low hills in the valley, I dreamed. I sat up and looked at myself sleeping.

Grandmother stood next to me, speaking urgently, "Child, listen to me! He's trying to kill you! He will murder you if you go away with him!" The sparkle in her eyes was replaced with dread and worry. "Please, child, listen to me!" She brought the hunting knife from behind her back. "He's going to kill you!"

Again I awoke, sweat pouring down my face and back. I shook and cried. Why could I not completely break from this man? I had years of professional training on how to escape and stay away from abusive relationships. I had talked numerous women out of them. And there I was, trapped, fear brimming out of me like a hot underground spring ready to explode into a geyser.

It had only been a few days since the last visit from Grandmother. The clock flashed red numbers: 1 a.m. I was in bed reading. A loud bang on the door made me drop the book. It was him! I looked around the room for an escape. The windows were too small. I was trapped!

I got to the front room just as he burst into my home, fury flashing across his face. "You're a cheating whore and I will kill you and take you out into these woods, bury you in a shallow grave, and no one will ever find you!"

He whipped out a hunting knife exactly like the one my grandmother had shown me. He pinned me to the bed and pushed the blade against my throat. I felt it cut through the first few layers of skin.

I don't know how long he held me there, but suddenly he let me up and wanted a cigarette. Maybe his addiction had taken a hold of him in his drunken state. Or maybe Grandmother and her friends were giving me one last chance to escape. I took it. Darkness was my ally as I slipped out the door, jumped into my car, and drove off. He chased me, getting in a couple of good punches on the side of my vehicle.

A couple of days later I returned with some friends and gathered my things. He was still in my life, but I somehow gained enough sense to live with other people. That controlled him for a little while. He never showed that abusive, cruel side in front of others. It was always one on one.

Grandmother soon returned. Her voice wasn't one of urgency, but of emergency. She stood very still, the purse hanging from her arm. "Please, child, if you go away with him he will kill you and bury you in that shallow grave, just like he promised! Please, listen to me!" I swear she trembled as her left hand reached out to me, fingers clutching the air as she faded away.

Now terrified, I listened. I moved, never giving away my location. He continued to hunt me, taking extremes to discover my location. I was still terrified that he would kill me. Persuaded by loved ones, I reported the events to the police and went for counseling at the Hays Caldwell Women's Center. They assisted me in getting a protective order. I was embarrassed and ashamed that I had allowed myself to become a victim of abuse, now being the one seeking help and refuge.

The man continued to stalk me and even spent time in jail for breaking the order. He is still around but completely out of my life. The embarrassment and shame have long gone. I share my story willingly so others may gain hope, faith, and courage to free themselves from abuse.

My grandmother stills comes to me annually, usually in December, the month of her birth and death. Her peaceful smile has returned and she continues to silently watch over me. With her guidance and the help of courageous friends, my life was spared an ill-fated end.

If you are so fortunate to have such a protector, listen and heed. It may save your life.

Denise Broussard has been intrigued with the paranormal since girlhood. Her life-long experiences have led her to become an active ghost hunter.

Being an avid rock hound, she uses stones when creating sacred space and in meditation and simply enjoys their unique beauty. A major portion of her collection can be attributed to Dan and Ginger Kiecke of the Broken Arrow Rock Shop in Wimberley, Texas.

While encouraged to delve deeper into writing and playing the flute by her mother, it was her father's experiences in Vietnam that inspired her to go into emergency medicine. A spider bite ended her career as a 911 field paramedic. She now devotes her time to prayer and family, including her son, who is in the military, and her German shepherd, Amethyst.

Denise studies comparative religion, philosophy, symbology, Native American cultures, gemology, and genealogy. Her diverse interests include falconry and pharology. She attends her local writing group, teaches meditation and spirit connection, and practices tai chi. She plans to travel and open a healing center for the abused.

She attributes her life to God as well as all the gifts that go with her chosen path. She believes in the healing qualities of prayer, the gifts of her wellness consultant, Elliot Sterling, Jr., the compassion and knowledge of her doctors, and the ongoing support of family and friends.

The Wimberley View published her essay "Finding Solace in the Power of Prayer." You can read her short story "Miracle on a Harley" at www.chivalrytoday.com. She loves writing horror and is an affiliate member of the Horror Writer's Association. Visit her web site at www.gemsandgenealogy.com.

Just a Breath Away

by J.M. Cornwell

During the years that one stroke after another took my grandmother away by inches, as she changed from a vibrant, sassy, intelligent, and loving woman into a shell that looked like her but whose eyes lacked the sparkle and simple joy of life, I went to see her less and less often. It's hard to lose someone in a senseless accident or after a protracted illness, but to watch the lighthouse of their mind dim slowly is worse.

Strokes took my grandmother's physical functions first, and each succeeding stroke took a little more of her mind until her body was reforged into a tightening fetal ball that could not be straightened. The gentlest and most loving touch tore her fragile skin and brought screams of pain. During the six years my grandmother existed in the nursing home, my mother went every evening to see her and sit and talk with her and I often went along. Age-dimmed blue eyes looked back at us with no recognition, on her face the smile of an infant to whom our faces and voices were a soft blur of colors and sounds. We reached out to her but she could not reach back to us, a prisoner of her deteriorating mind and weakening body.

The strokes continued to kill half of her brain and the doctors intervened time and again with tubes and medication, cutting holes in her body to force-feed her when the muscles in her throat ceased working, so they could keep her alive a little longer. Finally, when her body could take no more of their interventions, the doctors decided to take my grandmother off all the machines and let her die.

"My brother will be there," my mother said. "I think your grandmother would like it if you were there."

I could hardly keep the tears back as I answered, "My grandmother isn't there any more. She's gone."

"Well, I want you there."

I thought it over, trying to match the painfully thin and angular body with the strong and vibrant woman I had known all my life. "I don't want to be there. You're treating her death like some sort of circus attraction. I can't be there to watch."

"All right. Suit yourself," my mother's favorite final words. Suit myself. If I had suited myself I would never have let the doctors force-feed her or keep bringing her back from the brink of death to lie in a lonely bed among strangers.

The day the doctors took my grandmother off all the machines and took out all the wires and tubes, I stayed home and cried, unsure if I had made the right decision or if I was being selfish and disrespectful. What did Granny Good Witch, my name for my grandmother, want?

She wanted a quiet and simple funeral, and she made and paid for all the arrangements before her first stroke, right after my grandfather died. She wanted love and respect, and what was happening in that nursing home room wasn't loving or respectful, at least as far as I could see.

When the phone rang later that afternoon, I nearly jumped out of my skin. I knew before I picked up the phone who was calling.

"Mom slipped away peacefully. She's gone," my mother said, her voice breaking through her usually iron control.

"Thanks," I said to the sound of muffled sobs and hung up.

I knew my mother missed Granny Good Witch terribly and she always would. They had always been close and that was never more evident than watching my mother hold my grandmother's hand while Grandma looked up at her with unfocused innocent eyes, a sweet smile on her face, while Mom cried and said, "Mama, please don't leave me alone."

I didn't feel alone, but I had let my grandmother go many months before when she no longer recognized any of us. I felt that what had died that afternoon was the shell of my grandmother, not the woman with whom I spent so many happy afternoons together laughing and talking and cooking. I clung to those moments like a drowning woman clinging to a bit of wreckage in a storm-wracked sea.

I went to bed early that night, worn out from crying and unable to concentrate long enough to do anything productive. I tossed and turned, tried to read, and finally, a little after midnight by the nightstand clock, I fell asleep.

I don't remember any dreams. What I do remember is a light burning brighter and brighter against my eyelids. I sat up on the side of the bed, thinking I had forgotten to turn out the hall light, and went to the bedroom door. Groggily, I fumbled to open the door wider, reaching around the doorframe for the light, but it was off. I flipped the switch on and then off again, but the light persisted. I walked into the hall and saw a figured dressed in blue. It was my grandmother. She was wearing her favorite ankle-length smocked blue robe with the quilted mandarin collar. Shining with a soft white light, she stood there as if waiting for me to recognize her.

I couldn't stop the tears running down my cheeks as I reached out to her. She took my hands and held me closely, my chin grazing the soft halo of her silver hair, and patted my back while I cried.

"I'm sorry," I said between sobs," but I couldn't stand to be there today. I just couldn't watch."

"It's all right," she murmured. "I knew you were there for me even if you weren't in the room. It's all right."

Still holding her hands, I stepped back, and looked down at her as she smiled up at me. I didn't know what to say and I didn't want to let her go, but I knew I must, just as I had let her go when she no longer recognized me and I knew she wasn't coming back.

"I wanted to tell you something," she said. "I have always believed in you even though you don't believe in yourself. Believe in yourself and follow your heart and remember I'll always be just a breath away." And then she was gone.

When I woke the next morning I wasn't sure at first if I had dreamed that my grandmother was standing in the hall or if it had been real, but it didn't matter. I still felt her around me.

I went to the funeral three days later and went up to the coffin, not because it was expected but because I wanted to touch her one last time. Her body was straight again and she wore her favorite blue dress. I touched her cold cheek, but I knew she wasn't lying in that box; she was just a breath away.

J.M. Cornwell is a nationally syndicated journalist, security columnist, author, and book reviewer for both www.AuthorLink.com and www.thecelebritycafe.com. She was the professional editor and chief webmaster for award-winning *The Rose & Thorn* (www.theroseandthornezine.com) literary ezine until June 2004. She also designs the covers and illustrations for *The Rose & Thorn*. She

writes "Grammar Goofs," book reviews, and teaches character-
ization, humor, and writing at www.ScribeQuill.com, "Occam's
Razor," a paranormal column, for www.WhimsPlace.com, runs
Creative Ink, LLC, a professional editing service, and launched a
new magazine called *Living Voices* (http://livingvoices-
magazine.com) in December 2004.

She also writes book reviews for www.CurledUp-
Reviews.com, and is the new host of horror literature at Bella
Online (www.bellaonline.com/Site/horrorliterature). She lives in
the Colorado Rockies. Visit her blog on Blogger.

Not Quite an Accident

by Jan Bishop

I was just nine when my mother died. I didn't understand all the fuss when she was rushed to hospital at 3 a.m., nor did I understand when they came to tell me later that afternoon that she'd died. All I understood was that she supposedly wasn't coming back. I didn't want to ask if that meant just for the night, or was it a week that she'd be gone.

I went to bed that night still confused, so it wasn't surprising that when I woke in the early hours to find her hugging me, I was neither upset nor frightened. She sat on the edge of the bed as usual, her arms around me. Still half asleep, I hugged back. Then I looked up. Her eyes met mine in the moonlight and she spoke very softly.

"I'm so sorry, lovie. This is the last time you'll see me. Just remember I love you."

I was still sleepy and now bewildered. "Why do you have to go?"

"You'll understand when you're older. But I want you to remember I didn't leave you because I wanted to. It was your stepfather's fault. He sent me away." Her face twisted in sorrow. She hugged me again and stood up, bending to kiss my forehead. "Sleep tight."

I went to sleep again and when I woke up things had begun to change. I was sent to stay with friends of my mother's where I was not unhappy, but I missed my mother. I missed our cat and dog too. Silver, our big tabby, and Lassie, our foxy/spaniel cross, had been with me for years but now somehow they couldn't come to see me. My stepfather came once though, with a couple who thought they might like to adopt me. I glared.

"You made Mum go away. Why can't you bring her back?" His face paled slightly and he whisked the would-be adopters away.

He never came back, which didn't surprise me. I knew he hadn't really wanted me. I'd just been part of the package when my mother married him four years earlier. But he'd been familiar and so long as he visited I hoped he might bring Lassie and Silver. He couldn't have done that of course. I found out years later that he'd had both animals put down the day I was taken away.

Four months later I was adopted by another couple, while I wept in secret for my mother. I was badly abused by my new family for the next seven years until I was old enough to flee legally. Yet somehow, I never blamed my mother for abandoning me as I know other children have done. I could still recall the pain in her voice and the sadness of her expression. She hadn't wanted to leave me. Then when I was in my twenties I found out the truth about her death. My uncle was talking to me, and at last I asked questions someone would answer.

"What happened? No one ever told me how she died or why."

"It was a cerebral hemorrhage. You know she had bad headaches."

I remembered those. They'd send her to bed, crying with the pain, to lie in a darkened room all day taking aspirin and half-sleeping until the headache went away. The headaches had started about two years before her death. Now I listened to the rest of the story for the first time.

"The headaches got worse. She went to a doctor but he told her women got headaches and to take aspirin and lie down for a while. Then one didn't stop. It got worse and worse until she was delirious. They took her to hospital where the doctor there said it was a cerebral hemorrhage and they'd have to operate, but it was too late, she died on the operating table."

He looked sad about that. She'd been his favorite sister and he missed her too. I was quite simply furious at the doctor who'd seen her originally. If the fool had done something, then my mother might have survived. My uncle agreed.

"I know. I did speak to him afterward. He said she hadn't made it clear to him that the headaches were anything unusual."

"Unusual?"

"Yes, she had a fall down the front steps at your place. She hit her head and was knocked unconscious. The headaches started after that. The surgeon said that blow had done the damage. If she'd told her doctor about the fall, he might have done something before it was too late."

I was bitter. "All that from a fall? My stepfather couldn't wait to be rid of me once Mum died. He had Lassie and Silver killed, and dumped me on the first people who'd take me. Just from a stupid accident."

My uncle shook his head. "Not quite an accident," he said quietly. "Vera told me about it. They were arguing at the top of the steps and he pushed her."

I said nothing. I was remembering my mother's voice and her words. My stepfather had sent her away. She hadn't wanted to leave me; it was his fault she had to go. It all fit. I went away and cried then. Cried for my mother and my animals who'd paid the price for one man's temper. I wondered if he'd ever felt guilty over it.

I suspected, recalling his face when I'd asked him why he'd sent her away, that he'd known by then what the results of his action had been. One hasty, angry shove—that's all it took and a woman was dead, a child was alone. I doubt my mother haunted him; she wasn't the vengeful type. But for fifty years I've remembered her last visit and known that I was loved. It isn't enough to equal the years we could have had together, but it's something.

———————

Jan Bishop lives and works on New Zealand's North Island where she has a small sheep farm. Jan divides her time between the farm and her writing and, as Lyn McConchie, has had her short stories and books appear around the world including North America, Australia, Britain, Poland, and Russia. Her latest books, *Farming Daze* and *Daze On the Land* by Elizabeth Underwood (tales about her farm), have recently been published and are available on amazon.com.

Grandfather and the Wizard

by Paula Soto

My grandfather died when I was just seven years old. I can't say that I knew him very well, but I do have some fond memories of him. I remember his smiling face looking down at me as I sat on his lap, while we rocked back and forth in his favorite rocking chair. When all his grandchildren would come to visit, he would watch cartoons and play games with us for as long as we wanted. From flying kites to walking the dog, he was always involved in our activities. He made me feel happy, loved, and protected. Grandfather died of a heart condition, leaving behind his wife, five children, and numerous grandchildren, of which I was the youngest.

Our family had always been close, but after his death we seemed to grow closer. We started having family gatherings at Grandmother's house every weekend without fail. I think that spending so much time together helped ease everyone's pain. We all knew that we missed Grandfather greatly, but what we didn't know was that he missed us, too. Until the night an unforgettable thing happened.

It was a Saturday night. Most of our family members had been gathered together at Grandmother's house since early afternoon. We had all spent a long, enjoyable day—first playing a rousing game of baseball, then sitting down to the most delicious meal of meatloaf, mashed potatoes, and homemade biscuits I have ever tasted to this day. After our meal, the men flocked to the living room where the topics of sports and politics would dominate their conversation for the rest of the evening. The women migrated to the kitchen where they would wash the dishes and discuss their latest sewing projects. The children, as always, retired down the hallway to the last bedroom on the right. It had belonged to my Aunt Andrea when she had still lived at home with my grandparents, but had since become the room in which all the grandchildren spent the most time during their visits.

The bedroom was our favorite room in the house because of all it had to offer. It had the biggest television set, the biggest bed, and a chest full of Aunt Andrea's old toys, books, and board games she had left behind when she moved out. Next to the bedroom door was a vanity set complete with table, chair, and mirror that Grandmother had set up for any overnight guests who might occupy the room. On one side of the mirror, Grandmother had attached a couple of hooks on which to hang a key ring, purse, or other small item. Being a Catholic woman, Grandmother had hung a rosary on one of the hooks.

We had been in the room for about ten minutes when one of my cousins, after having consulted the local television listings, announced that our favorite movie of all time was about to begin: *The Wizard of Oz*. The room fell silent. It was a sentimental moment for all of us. It was not only our favorite movie, but it had also been Grandfather's favorite movie. In fact, every time it had been scheduled to air on television, he would give us a call and say, "Don't forget to watch the wizard." We all loved to watch it, and even though Grandfather was gone, tonight was no exception. So, we shut off the lights, made ourselves comfortable, and turned the channel to the right station.

About forty-five minutes had passed, and we were watching the movie quietly and undisturbed. I sat upright on the bed with a pillow behind my back separating my body from the wooden headboard. My older sister sat next to me in the same manner. My cousin Anita lay on the bed on her stomach with her elbows propped up beneath her. My other four cousins sat on the floor next to the bed atop a small mountain of pillows. The bedroom door was ajar about an inch. The hallway was dark and empty, but if we listened carefully during the commercials, we could hear our parents' voices on the other side of the house. It sounded as if the women had finished cleaning up in the kitchen and had joined the men in the living room. At one point, I heard Grandmother say something about a fork, but I couldn't quite make out her exact words.

I never would have believed what happened next if I had not been there. Out of nowhere, I had a sudden feeling of coldness all around me. The windows were closed and the air conditioner was not on, yet I felt a chill even through the thickness of my fleece pullover. I folded my arms against my chest to try to warm myself, but the cold feeling would not go away. Then, my sister leaned next to my ear and whispered, "Look at the rosary." I did as she said, and looked in the direction of the vanity mirror and the hooks attached to it. From one of the hooks was the rosary, not hanging motionless as it had been earlier, but tapping itself steadily against the mirror! It moved as if someone held the rosary and was purposely tapping its plastic beads against the glass, except that none of us were near enough to even touch it.

I grabbed my sister's arm as we watched and listened to the sound of the tapping beads. Anita became aware of the sound, and then the three of us were watching the rosary dance. Then the tapping suddenly stopped, and before we could say anything, the bedroom door slowly creaked itself wide open. I looked toward the open doorway and there in the darkness, I saw a familiar figure standing tall. It was Grandfather looking into the room, with the same big smile on his face that he always used to wear. He wasn't moving around much, just hovering silently in the doorframe. Without warning, Anita let out a long, high shriek, and instantaneously Grandfather disappeared.

In a few seconds the hallway light came on, followed by our parents' footsteps. They entered the bedroom and flicked on the light switch to see what all the commotion was about. Grandmother followed behind them with a concerned look on her face. "It was Grandpa's ghost! It was Grandpa's ghost! Didn't you all see it? And the rosary, it moved!" shouted Anita. My sister and I nodded our heads, while the rest of our cousins said they didn't see anything. I later realized that they hadn't seen anything because they had been sitting on the floor. The height of the bed had blocked their view of the door as well as the vanity. After hearing my sister, Anita, and I tell the same story of what we had witnessed, our parents tried to reassure us. They told us that Grandfather just missed us terribly and wanted to be with us again. They said there was nothing to be afraid of, and that we would all say extra prayers for Grandfather at church services the next morning. Grandmother smiled at us and nodded in agreement with tears in her eyes.

A few days later, I learned from my mother that Grandmother had had a ghostly encounter of her own the same day that we saw Grandfather in the doorway. That morning, she had been tidying up the kitchen before any family members had arrived. She had just finished washing her breakfast dishes, which consisted of a plate, coffee cup, and fork. She not only washed the three items but dried them and put them away in their proper places. When she had finished, she started walking down the hallway toward her bedroom to do a bit of knitting. She was halfway down the hall when she heard a noise in the kitchen. She said it sounded as if a utensil had been dropped. She turned and headed back toward the kitchen. Upon entering, she did not see anything out of place at first glance. Then, her eyes caught sight of it. There on the counter next to the sink, was a fork. Knowing she had put all the dishes away, Grandmother walked over to the counter and picked up the fork. She gasped. It was the same fork she had used at breakfast, except that it was definitely not washed and dried. The teeth of the fork were moist, and dangling from the tips of the teeth were a few small strands of what looked like saliva.

Grandmother said that when Grandfather was alive he would always get a fork, and use it to take a bite of whatever Grandmother had on her plate, even if he had already cleaned his own plate. Then, he would give her a wink and say that hers tasted better. After telling my mother her story, Grandmother said that she knew it was just Grandfather's way of keeping up his old habits, and letting her know that he was still around.

Paula Soto has been writing creatively since she was a child. In her teens, she actively contributed to her school newspaper as an editor, and to her school literary club as a regular contributing writer of short stories and poetry. In college, she majored in English, with an emphasis in creative writing, in which she further studied novel writing, short story writing, poetry writing, scriptwriting, and playwriting. She has studied American, British, and French literature, among literature of other origins.

In addition to writing, Paula considers her great loves to be reading, animals, traveling, music, and the Internet. She has traveled to various locations around the globe, with her most recent trip to Miami, Florida. She has a deep appreciation of all types of music, but calls rock music as her favorite. The youngest of three daughters, Paula was born in 1970 in Southern California, where she grew up. She currently lives in Los Angeles.

Joe

by Karen A. Carpenter

I was barely twenty-one when I met the man who would become the best male friend I've ever had. Joe was only nineteen, and his friendship was exactly what I needed back then. I'd always preferred the company of men, but all too often, that inevitable something popped up and doomed a perfectly good platonic relationship.

Joe freed me from such concerns. Joe was gay. And though he undoubtedly dragged me off to more gay men's clubs than I care to remember, I would not trade one second of our time together for anything.

We often danced the night away in those clubs. And though, while we were dancing, Joe inevitably collected a dizzying assortment of names and telephone numbers for future use, he never forgot that I was his date for the evening.

Joe was into all the latest crazes, always searching for different experiences. That could mean finding a new sexual partner, attending a mind control course, or even just playing the latest in-vogue games. Backgammon was all the rage back then, for reasons I've never understood. Yet I could endlessly play the game with Joe. We would stare at that stupid board for hours, laughing continuously at nothing in particular. Having Joe in my life was a blessing, though I did discover early on that he had a reckless, irresponsible side. But so what? We were young. And indestructible.

We worked at the same company. Joe was that rare kind of work friend that I enjoyed being with outside of work. We confided in each other. A crazed ex-boyfriend of mine became quite a problem in my life. The maniac stalked me and threatened to kill me. Long after the situation was resolved, even after I suspected that this ex-boyfriend was dead, my nightmares about him continued. Joe was always there to listen to my tales of woe and to help whenever he could.

To drown our troubles, we often indulged in cocktails at lunchtime. In a pub full of straight people. Without the distractions of potential sexual partners, Joe's spiritual side emerged. Especially in regard to the friction between Joe and his father. Joe's dad had difficulty accepting his son's sexuality. And Joe was so strong-willed and stubborn, he couldn't tolerate anyone who didn't immediately accept him for exactly who he was.

I often offered neutral advice. But all too frequently, Joe shut me out, burying his pain even deeper.

One night, during a party at Joe's house, Joe and his father argued over the phone. I followed up that call with a stern lecture to Joe about being more understanding toward his dad. "You never know when it will be too late," I emphasized.

Joe grumbled and basically told me to mind my own business.

Hours later, Joe's dad was dead.

Joe later reminded me of the lecture I'd given him after that call. I'd actually forgotten about what I'd said, but my comments had left an impression on Joe. And yet his resentments still lingered.

Months later, during one of our trouble-drowning sessions in the pub, the issues between Joe and his dad resurfaced. Joe had recently graduated from one of his infamous mind control courses. He was spouting all these wild theories about how he could finally make everything all right with his father. "It's too late," I reminded my friend, probably adding a few *I told you so* innuendoes.

But Joe was convinced that he could still reach out to his dad. His latest seminar had taught him a method of altering the energy between people. And energy never died; this method supposedly worked backward and forward, across time and space.

I didn't buy into the theory, but respectfully nodded every now and then. But when Joe got to the part about how he had to retreat into his imaginary closet to perform these alterations, I actually laughed out loud. I couldn't help myself. I made stupid jokes like, "You've always been out of the closet, why in the world would you need to go into one now?"

This was one time I couldn't make my old backgammon buddy laugh. I'd never seen him more serious. He swore that while he was in that confined closet space of his imagination, he could fix everything that had ever been wrong between him and his father. All he had to do was hold an image of his father in his mind, and his dad would be right there with him. In that closet.

I nearly knocked my drink over. "Why can't you guys meet in a scenic park or something?" I taunted.

Joe explained that the spiritual energy meeting could really take place anywhere. The closet method happened to work for him. For the healing to take place, one has to imagine himself and the other person being bathed in a powerful, loving, bright light. Eventually, that visualization will transform any negative energy.

I had always believed in the power of the mind. Yes, I did admit that this method might possibly work, but only if all the people involved were still alive. I believed it was impossible to influence someone this way when that someone was dead.

This subject came up several more times. We inevitably disagreed. But Joe was always so sure. I assumed his adamancy stemmed from the guilt he must have felt over that not-so-pleasant final conversation with his father. Maybe he needed to convince me that he'd found a way to get beyond all that. And then, he probably wouldn't have minded throwing in a few *I told you so*'s of his own.

Never coming to any sort of an agreement, we eventually dropped the issue. Besides, Joe insisted that he'd taken care of everything… in his closet.

Time passed. Neither one of us brought it up again.

More time passed and one day we realized that it had been ages since we'd danced till dawn in the clubs. When had we suddenly stopped being so wild and carefree?

I married. Joe and his lover moved in together. But Joe could never stabilize that powerful streak of irresponsibility that coursed through his veins. No longer cloaked within the supposed indestructibility of youth, his reckless nature began causing serious problems. He was fired from his job. My lunch buddy of ten years was no more.

His negligence over other issues alienated even me. We drifted apart. Months passed and neither of us attempted to make contact. Eventually, through a mutual friend, I learned the truth that I had feared the most: Joe had AIDS.

I pushed all petty grievances aside and reunited with my old buddy. But still, certain feelings of resentment haunted me. I couldn't comprehend how Joe could have done this to himself. And worse, how many other people had his mindless sexual encounters killed along the way? His faithful, monogamous lover, for one.

Nightmares of Joe infiltrated my sleep. I saw him stalking the dark city streets, slashing unsuspecting men to death. I'd always believed that friends needed to talk about issues in order to resolve them. But how could I tell my buddy this? How could I possibly break it to a dying man that I sometimes thought of him as a vicious serial killer? These dreams of Joe only added to my nighttime stress, as I was still being haunted by nightmares of my crazy stalker ex-boyfriend.

I visited Joe, yes, but not as often as I should have. Joe ended up living longer than anyone had anticipated. Unfortunately, this unforeseen gift of time, combined with my feelings of resentment, lulled me into a false sense of security. I honestly believed Joe had more time.

Our final conversation took place on the phone. Joe sounded absolutely desperate. "Come see me," he pleaded. "Don't shy away from me like everyone else. Please!"

I wanted to see him, but I did have some issues to work out. And I was soooooo busy. While I was still struggling with my doubts, Joe quietly slipped out of this world.

Though I had preached to Joe about treasuring the time with your loved ones, I hadn't heeded my own advice. And now, ironically, I'd been left to struggle with the guilt of that final phone call, just as Joe had anguished over his last conversation with his father.

All resentments I'd had toward Joe vanished. Depression rushed in to fill the void. Why hadn't I been able to put my personal judgments aside sooner? This wasn't anything like the tragedy of Joe's father, when a sudden heart attack snatched that robust man right off of the tennis court. I knew Joe was dying.

After the funeral, I stayed in bed for several days. Drifting in and out of a troubled sleep, I kept hearing a distant telephone. I forced myself out of bed several times to answer it, but then the ringing would always stop. There were never any messages on the answering machine.

I'd doze off and it would start again. It rang endlessly on and on and on. I realized, finally, that it had to be a dream phone. And for some reason, I did not want to take that call. Why wouldn't it stop? The ringing grew louder. More insistent. Then I spotted him. Joe! He held a telephone in his hand.

"I'm not answering," I called out. I already had too many phantoms haunting my dreams. Joe gestured for me to pick up the phone. He looked peaceful... almost angelic. White light and heavenly clouds surrounded him.

Please make the ringing stop.

"What do you want?" I hollered. He gestured again toward the phone. I knew my stubborn old buddy would haunt me forever if I didn't grant him the final word.

I grabbed the receiver. "WHAT?"

Joe didn't say a word. He pointed down at something. The ringing stopped. Then, in one angelic sweep of his magic wand fingers, and with a peaceful, wise look upon his face, he became one with the heavenly clouds.

What was that all about?

I looked down to where he'd been pointing. I spotted a park bench. Suddenly, I was on that bench. And my crazy ex-boyfriend was beside me. For the first time in ages, the vision of this man in my dream didn't scare me half to death. The man who had once nearly murdered me, looked at me and smiled. I hesitantly smiled back. We sat together for a few minutes, when suddenly bright sunlight immersed us in its glow. It beamed down on us and I felt utterly bathed in peace and love. Such rapturous, wondrous light. This was heaven. I know. Sheer bliss and love and understanding and forgiveness. My ex gently wrapped his arm around me and I rested my head on his shoulder. It felt so natural. So right.

Eventually, the sun subsided. We left the park and I took a short walk with my wonderful, loving, ex-boyfriend. We were both still aglow with celestial light. After a few moments, my heavenly friend turned and smiled and began walking away. I wasn't certain where he was headed, but I knew it was not for me to follow. I watched, waving good-bye, until he, and the city block where he walked, became one with the clouds.

Leave it to Joe. Coming through like that with a symbolic phone call. Our truly final telephone exchange. His message was so crystal clear and cleansing and loving for all of us. Joe transformed all of our negative energies, on that remarkable park bench, with his loving gift of light. He didn't even need to present his image inside that light. Actually, Joe always did prefer his personal closet method. And I'm certain that he knew better than to invite me in there.

My nightmares disappeared, never to return. Just like when we'd first met, when I'd yearned for an intimate, platonic friendship, Joe had once again given me exactly what I needed.

Knowing my stubborn old buddy though, he had at least one ulterior motive up his magical sleeve. He probably plans on taking me to lunch some day in his favorite, afterlife pub in the sky. Maybe we'll once again feel like dancing the night away. Or maybe we'll just sit and talk. But sooner or later, probably when I least expect it, he'll bring up the subject of his closet and the light. And then, eeeeeekkkkk, I can almost hear it now....

"Karen. I told you so."

Karen Ann Carpenter is an extremely versatile writer. Her fiction can be charming, funny, scary, sensual, philosophical, or . . . gross! She'll take a break from writing a gruesome horror story to create a magical fairytale land for children — or to perfect an apple pie recipe for her holiday cooking newsletter, *Celebrate The Now*. Karen also writes non-fiction articles that highlight the eerie and mysterious possibilities of life. She lives in New Jersey with her husband, and their black Labrador Retriever, Buddy. Visit Karen on the web at KarenAnnCarpenter.com.

The Afghan

by Sharman Horwood

"What a remarkable woman!" I was very enthusiastic. My friend was not. "Mrs. Leidecker. Wasn't she amazing?"

Stephanie laughed at me. "Not really. She was just an old woman with a lot of stories." Stephanie didn't have an ounce of imagination in her. In that respect we were opposites, yet very close, so close we often finished the other's sentences.

"So? Some older women…."

"Know things," she finished, turning to look at me. My hand automatically reached for the door handle. But she quickly looked back at the road, smiling. She was a good driver and knew it.

Her eyes were steady on the next stoplight as she continued. "Mrs. Leidecker does know things, particularly who's going to believe her." She grinned, adding, "She tells stories as well as you do." In that much Stephanie was correct.

That afternoon, Mrs. Leidecker had sat, sedately British, on Mrs. Caroll's living room sofa. "Ghosts are real," Mrs. Leidecker had announced, her accent clear and precise when the discussion turned to ghost stories, "just as real as you or me." I don't remember how the subject came up but we all leaned in, enthralled. From the doorway, Stephanie rolled her eyes, a wry grin teasing the ends of her mouth. "We'd gone for the summer to Newquay in Cornwall." Across the room, Mr. Leidecker nodded agreeably in his chair, a white-haired gentleman with a moustache and ruddy cheeks. The pair looked every bit their generation of British travellers.

"Instead of staying at a B & B," she continued, "we rented a cottage for two weeks. A very pretty one, with a rose garden and arbor where we could sit outside on hot afternoons. But the first night we were there, I woke to a noise downstairs."

Her husband, apparently, hadn't heard it, but did when she'd nudged him awake: "There was something there. Not sure what, but definitely something."

She beamed before going on. "When we went downstairs, we didn't find anything, no door or window unlatched, and certainly no intruders. So we jotted it up to imagination, didn't we, Arthur?" He agreed, still smiling. My impression was that they were a happy couple, well used to each other's ways.

"But we were wrong. I went to the greengrocer's the next day. The storekeeper asked where we were staying. 'Not the Ramsey cottage?' she asked, eyes wide. 'There's ghosts there,' she said, 'as sure as I'm standing here.' Previous tenants claimed they'd been visited nightly, supposedly by the ghost of a man who'd lost his wife to the sea."

Her husband broke in quickly: "Drowned, she did. Wicked storms there in the winter. She went for a walk one night and didn't come home. Her body was found on the shingle a week later." He sat comfortably back in his chair. He'd said his piece.

Mrs. Leidecker took up the tale again. "Her husband never forgave himself. And after he died his ghost kept coming back to the cottage, looking for her. Still does." She nodded, her hands clasped gently across her middle.

"Really?" I was lapping up every bit of this story. I loved ghost stories, especially true ones. But I didn't dare meet Stephanie's eye, not until we had a chance to talk about it later.

"So you saw it?" There was a gleam in Stephanie's eyes. I didn't think it was interest on her part. She wanted more fuel to tease me with after everyone had left.

But the Leideckers were quite happy to oblige. "Go on, Mother. Tell them about it." Mr. Leidecker was thoroughly enjoying himself. He leaned over to help himself to another bit of cake, lodging it in the saucer of his teacup.

She looked around at us. "Are you sure?" I wasn't the only one to nod enthusiastically.

"Well, then. It happened one night while Arthur was in town. His mother was quite ill, and he'd taken the train in to visit her. I had the children so I stayed in the cottage. I kept them at the beach all day—I didn't want them to know how worried we were." She looked over at her husband. He briefly, and quite seriously, looked down at his tea. His mother hadn't survived.

His wife went on. "That night I couldn't sleep. The children were tired out and went off to bed with the promise of another day at the beach if the good weather held up. I sat up in bed and read for a while, but the light wasn't good, and I was almost as tired as the children." She smiled, fondly. She hadn't talked about her children, although I realized that one of them was in the room with us. Her son.

"I didn't get to sleep for quite some time. It was so quiet outside, more quiet than I was used to in the city. And I was worried about Arthur's mother, of course. Eventually I drifted off to sleep. When I woke, it was the middle of the night. There was no moon and the room was very dark. No streetlights, only starlight outside the window. I couldn't see anything." She paused. "But I also couldn't move. Something was holding my legs down." She pressed her hands into her lap to show us.

"I couldn't get up. I couldn't even shift my knees enough to turn away from the weight. I felt around with my hands but nothing was there. It was like a big dog or a body was laying across me, pinning me to the bed. Well, I never." She shook her head. "I'd not felt anything like that before. Had something gone wrong with my legs? Like paralysis for some reason?

"But I felt my toes all right. I could wiggle them. So it couldn't be anything like that. Eventually, I just got so angry that I shouted, 'Get off me!' And it moved. I still couldn't really see anything, but there was just enough starlight for me to see a shimmer, like a transparent figure with eyes lit by the stars for a split second. Then it was gone. And it didn't come back. Arthur was back the next day so I was never alone again, but I'll not forget it, that's for sure."

I too didn't forget. I didn't see Mrs. Leidecker again; unfortunately, Arthur had a heart attack a few days later, and when she returned to England, she took him with her for his funeral there. A terrific couple, and a hard way for their holiday to end.

At the time, just as I'd expected, Stephanie teased me about believing the story. "You know it's not true. If there are ghosts, there's no reason for them to come back and haunt people. It's just people's imagination," she scoffed.

"There are ghost stories in every culture around the world," I shot back. "That wouldn't be so if these things didn't happen." Even my mother had a story of her own, but I wasn't about to add that one to the discussion. Stephanie would literally throw her hands up then.

But she didn't change her mind. "It doesn't make sense. If the man's wife died, then he later died, and there's life after death, why wouldn't he see her then? Why does he have to come back to this world to look for her?"

"So you're saying if one of us died before the other, you wouldn't come back to talk to me?" I grinned. I didn't mean it, of course. It was just a point I was trying to make.

She grinned right back. "Like that's about to happen." We were both in our early twenties. We had lifetimes ahead of us. We planned to fill them with children and grandchildren, then grow old together in the same neighborhood. Our husbands realized they'd probably have no say in this.

Stephanie continued. "No, I'd probably wait around for you to call me. That's what you're likely to do." She was right. Stephanie rarely had to call me. I was usually the first to pick up the phone and dial.

Mrs. Leidecker's story stayed with me. She'd spoken so matter-of-factly, and with so much conviction. Her tale had to be true.

Christmas was just around the corner. It was Stephanie's first anniversary as well. We both liked to make things. At that time, I loved embroidery and needlepoint; Stephanie spent hours knitting afghans. I think we were both working on our homemaking skills before children and careers filled up our lives. For her gift, I embroidered a needlepoint picture of flowers: purple and pink pansies clutched in a bouquet. When she handed me a large parcel in return, I hoped it was an afghan. It was. It glowed in autumn-rich colours—yellows, golds, and rust—and would look perfect on the back of my living room couch. It was thick and warm, but no one was going to use it. No spilt coffee or messy dog hair was going to ruin this. It was too precious.

"I can knit you another," she told me, surprised and yet pleased that I valued it as much as I did.

"It wouldn't be the same," I pointed out. "It wouldn't be this one." I felt there'd never be another one, and I'd been thrilled she'd taken so much time to make something for me. That was what made it special. She hadn't just gone and bought it. She'd picked out the colours she knew I'd like, and even though it had taken her two months, she'd worked on it every evening after work. That was why it meant so much. Stephanie always knew what would please me. More than husband or family, she knew.

So for years, that afghan stayed on the couch. I thought of her every time I looked at it.

But one cold night, Stephanie left us.

I didn't know until the phone rang the next morning. It was Mrs. Caroll, Stephanie's mother.

"Are you on your own?" she began. "I have some terrible news."

I was. My husband was working the night shift, and wasn't home yet.

"It's OK," I told her. "He'll be here soon. What's wrong?" I felt extremely cold. Something terrible had happened. And somehow I knew, even before she said the words.

"I'm afraid Stephanie is gone," she told me. "It was her heart. A tear in a valve that went last night. There was nothing the doctors could do." She was sobbing.

I couldn't catch my breath. My legs felt heavy, like I'd been struck down.

"No!" I cried. I heard the front door. My husband had just come in. "No!" I cried out again. "It's not possible!" I tried to move my legs, but I couldn't shift them under the blankets. Like something held them down.

"It was sudden," Mrs. Caroll went on. "She didn't suffer. She was gone before they even got to the hospital." She must have heard Ben at the door. "Are you still alone?"

"No," I told her. "Ben's here." My breath clogged my throat. The pain in my chest was so deep, I ached like I'd been sucker-punched.

And my legs were still heavy, inert. I looked down.

The afghan lay across them. Even as my eyes fell on it, the weight lifted, and I felt nothing more than the normal pressure of the bedspread on my knees.

I barely heard Mrs. Caroll say she'd call later. Nor do I remember hanging up the phone, or what I said to Ben. All I could see was the afghan, draped across my legs.

I hadn't put it there. Last night the afghan had been where it always was: on the back of the couch, beautiful and untouched.

Nor was it heavy enough to be the weight I'd felt.

Stephanie had come to say good-bye. She hadn't waited for my call after all.

Sharman Horwood is a science fiction/fantasy writer who teaches ESL in Seoul, South Korea. Her first published short story is in *Catfantastic IV,* and she has written a textbook published in Korea for ESL, titled *North American Discussions of Today.* She has published short pieces in *Horse Dreams*, as well as *Canadian Animals Are Smarter Than Jack*. In between writing two novels, one of which is a sequel to an Andre Norton novel, she has also collaborated on an alternate history novel, *Queen of Iron Years*, with New Zealand writer Lyn McConchie.

The Phantom Swimmer

by Jo Franklin

I am not a wealthy person. However, I always feel that there should be something in a person's life that is a bit of an extravagance. For my neighbour, it is an expensive hairdo "costing her the earth" every few weeks. For my husband, it is the wines that he stocks carefully in the garden shed and hardly ever drinks. And for me? Well—it's my private health club, not too far away, of which I have been a member for some time.

I love everything about it—well, perhaps not quite everything. The gym—that makes me feel grumpy. When I do my workout other people, including the gym instructor, smile and scratch their heads. I'm not keen on organised exercise; perhaps it's too reminiscent of school for me, with the strict teacher expecting me to do this, that, and the other. I have always been gawky, with two left feet. I could never understand things like sports day. Trying to jump over a hurdle whilst trying to run was a total disaster. My brain could never convince the rest of me that I should sail up into the air like a gazelle and then come gracefully down to earth. Ungracefully—that would be more like me.

However, when I discovered water rather later than most people, this was a different kettle of fish—excuse the pun! I had a thing about water. It fascinated me. It seemed so sensual. I would sit looking longingly at the water and the way people swished through it. They were its master. But I was not its master, not to begin with. It took me ages just to get into the jacuzzi, and getting into the swimming pool was one of the great challenges of my life, although it was only about a metre deep and comparatively safe. I found a good teacher, but it still took me a long time to learn. However, my confidence grew, and eventually I could swim the entire length of the pool—with the right conditions of course. None of this head-under-the-water business. There must be no energetic swimmers to make the water choppy and no frivolous people talking in high voices to put me off. I was happy. I had achieved something. I was a weak swimmer but I had succeeded. The water was no longer in charge and everything was fine. I did a swim most weeks; could use the pools on holiday; could share the fun in the sea.

But then things went wrong. I had a major operation. For weeks I could concentrate only on walking. I grew stronger and finally returned to my club, fully recovered. But horrors! I could get into the pool, but the water seemed like my enemy, threatening to drown me. It churned against me and tried to cover me. I could no longer launch myself into the swimming position. However much I tried to persuade them, my legs would not leave the bottom. I felt heavy; the water was alien. My confidence had completely gone. My only salvation was that I could swim with a float. If my arms had something to hang on to, I could get my feet off the bottom and use my legs. But I could no longer swim. I felt depressed and miserable. The whole thing was a disaster.

Just a few weeks ago, I went to the club early in the afternoon. It's a good time to go because it can be comparatively empty. It was quiet—not many people in the changing rooms, no one in the jacuzzi. As I sat in the jacuzzi I noticed the spray from the water. I suppose it must be there all the time, but I hadn't noticed it quite like this before. There was a mist that rose into the air. The droplets formed a curtain and it was impossible to see through it. It was incredibly beautiful, and incredibly mysterious. It made me feel calm, pensive, content.

I left the jacuzzi and peered through the glass door into the swimming pool area. Again, it was empty. The water was as calm as the feeling in me. There were no ripples, no sounds, apart from the distant rhythm of some quiet music. I remember taking a float and going into the pool. The steps down were crystal clear; the only way to distinguish each was by the line at the edge of each. I danced down them in time to the music—not like me at all. The feel of the water was beautiful. It was cool and welcoming.

I started to swim. The float led the way, my hands lay gently on it. My legs kicked at the water behind me in a slow methodical way. I was almost halfway down the pool when I heard someone swimming behind me. I carried on. But the swimmer was persistent. I slowed down, expecting to be overtaken. I could see the water lapping at the side, hear the swimmer—and yet I had not heard the door open to the swimming pool. I was certain no one had come in, still, I must have been wrong. I stopped and turned. There was no swimmer behind me! There was no one to be seen. I was completely alone. Taken aback, I swam on, slowly, listening. But the sound of anyone behind me had gone. There was no one else. The swish of the water against the side of the pool was the only thing I could hear.

So who was the phantom swimmer? There was someone who occasionally used the club in the mid-1990s, who died tragically young. Someone I used to see swimming with such ease and grace that I could only stand by the side of the pool in awe. She moved through the water as though she was a part of it, a way I could never understand. She used to smile at me, and nod, as if to say, *come on, it's easy, just follow me*. And then they told us one day at the club that she was gone. She had been killed in a terrible car wreck. Was that my phantom swimmer? Come back for just one more swim? I'll never know, will I? Strangely enough, after that day I found I could swim again.

Jo Franklin has written many short stories on such subjects as crime, science fiction, and romance. Recently she was published twice in U.K.'s prestigious *Writing Magazine*—winning first prize in the Science Fiction Short Story 2003 competition and first prize in the Crime Short Story 2004 competition. This is her second published story with Atriad Press. Jo has also written three novels. From a very early age she has had an empathy for the spiritual world, and has had some experiences that are hard to explain. Jo lives in beautiful Berkshire, England, with her husband, Roger, and her grey cat, Tigger. Her web site is www.JoFranklin.com, and she welcomes visitors.

Judy

by Joan Scott

Easter Sunday dawned fresh. We made plans to take Grandma on a boat ride to celebrate this beautiful day. While she showered I sipped my second cup of coffee and read the newspaper in the kitchen. The holiday ham and all its trimmings rested in the refrigerator. My husband worked on his laptop. When doesn't he? My teenagers were in their bedrooms, computers whirring, radios blaring. Your average Sunday.

The telephone rang. A call from Seattle. It was Bill, husband of my best friend Judy. His somber voice told me he had bad news. I made a quick, panicked inventory. Had something happened to one of my family members? No, of course not. They were all here with me. Grandma had flown down from Seattle last week. Then what? Judy. Oh, my God.

"You need to sit down, Joanie," he said. It sounded like a movie script. I sat, feeling numb. "There's been an accident. Judy and Dorothy." Dorothy was Judy's mother and my mother's best friend. My heart thumped in my chest. "They were driving in the rain and hit a bus."

"Are they OK?" I asked. As if they would be.

"No, Joanie. They're both dead."

It couldn't be true. It didn't compute. I saw the car in my mind's eye. It spun in circles. Odd though, it was happening not in the Pacific Northwest, but in California, where my mother had a close call years ago. Strange, the images that come to mind. I

194

told Bill I didn't believe him, a quick defense of the mind and heart.

"It's true, Joanie."

"Oh, Bill." My heart went out to him. I agonized for my mother, for me.

We talked a bit longer, two zombies finding our way in the haze. I stood up. And hung up. To this day, my kitchen chair holds the memory of that moment.

I walked—or maybe staggered—to my husband's office. I had two thoughts: to turn this over to him, since I couldn't deal with it. (And that's not me—I'm strong), and to make this go utterly away before my mother emerged from her shower. I had only minutes. Because it might kill her, too, and I couldn't live without her. Isn't it interesting how protecting our loved ones is all about self-interest? We keep them alive and then we get to stay alive.

In the end, I told her. I had no other choice.

We went for our boat ride anyway, telling ourselves life goes on. But it wasn't the same. My mother sat in the back of the boat, weeping. My children's faces showed how they agonized for their grandmother. Mother Nature told us to glorify this beautiful day. Instead we wept.

I remembered the last time I saw Judy. Only six weeks ago. After much nagging on my part, she came to Fort Worth. It wasn't as if she didn't love me. She probably couldn't afford it. And she was busy at her new job. She had just finished her degree in architecture at the University of Washington—at the young age of fifty-five. She had worked so hard, pulling regular "all-nighters" to garner her degree. She loved the rewards, and had earned them. She raised two fine young men as well. Handsome. Nice. An insipid word, but true. Really decent human beings. Now Judy was free to savor life.

The morning after she arrived, Judy ate breakfast while I finished up work. Then I took the rest of the day off. We worked out at the club, had lunch, and shopped.

The next day we went to Dallas. After sharing a latte or two, we visited one of those chic little cooking shops. She bought me an apron that said "Shitake Happens." Doesn't it, though? At dusk, we stopped at a trendy little bar and restaurant and had a cosmopolitan—watching all the young people scope each other out. Like we used to do in our younger, more beautiful, club-hopping days. And Judy was beautiful then. And she was still. What cheekbones. Oh, those days, they were grand.

I kept tight control over my liquor consumption. After all, I had to get my Judy back home in one piece. I didn't want to get into an accident. After my cosmopolitan I drank a glass of wine with dinner. Two hours later I felt quite sober. Judy, usually a model of restraint when it came to alcohol, had decided she was on vacation. She deserved it. She had a couple more glasses of wine, growing more charming by the minute. More power to her, my hard-working, fun-loving, beautiful Judy. Taking a break. As we drove back to Fort Worth, I searched my mind for a place to cap off the night in festive style—the city has few. We stopped at a yuppie enclave. I wanted something elegant, and Judy had another drink. I ordered mineral water. Just to be safe.

I remember the drive home. We sang silly songs from our youth, Judy setting the pace, me just driving. Naughty songs about Hitler and places in Eastern Washington with names like Walla Walla. "I wanna walla in Walla Walla, cause Walla Walla's my home town." The moon high, the sunroof open—and Judy in rare form. It was girlfriendness in its most satisfying shape.

It was all there would be.

When I took her to the airport the next day, we hugged good-bye. I watched her board the plane. Rugged, forthright, soft. Herself. "Good-bye, Judy. Good-bye." I had no idea it would be the last time. "Turn around, Judy, and wave good-bye just once more. I love you so much." She didn't look back again. I wanted her to—just one last time.

But later she did—after she was gone forever. Whenever I have a burning question, I ask Judy. And I feel her hovering around my shoulders giving me her answer. She believed in spirituality. She once lived in the Orient, and brought back its mysticism with her. Now she is all spirit.

Her father says when they are gone they are just gone. Not for me. How can I have a pipeline he doesn't have, as close as he was to the two of them? But I do. Girlfriend stuff. I see the little brown spots on Judy's left wrist. I see her mother's thinning hair, lovely hands, pretty nails. I hear Dorothy's voice, Judy's voice—low and soft like Mary Travers of Peter, Paul, and Mary.

And they are always with me. Literally. Call me crazy. All through my time on this planet, when I have not known what to do about this thing we call life I have asked God, about whom I am usually nonchalant, for His guidance. And He has given it. Now I receive it through Judy. She taught me to live my life to its fullest because she never got to finish hers.

She tells me, speaking right over my shoulder, not to fear. To heck with terrorism. Do it right now, before you are too old to get on the tour bus. If they shoot you, they shoot you. Better to die thumbing your nose at them than to die of boredom. Better quick death than slow. I remembered that when I visited South Africa and Australia and New Zealand shortly after her death.

She had a saying. It was essential Judy and my new mantra: "There will be only one of you for all time. Be yourself fearlessly." Yes!

Joan Scott makes her living as a freelance writer. Her articles have appeared at wineandcuisine.org and in *Distinctive Lifestyles* magazine, *Where, Key, Restaurant Forum*, and *Chile Pepper*. She has also written for the *Fort Worth Star-Telegram*, *Greensboro News and Record*, and *Senior News*. Joan has received several awards for her marketing communications and nonfiction writing. She is currently at work on a memoir. Joan lives in Fort Worth, Texas, with her husband and man's best friend.

In the Dark of the Night

by Linda Ruzicka

Sometimes in the dark maelstrom of life, you reach up over the pit's edge hoping for rescue. You never know who or what is going to grab your hand.

When I was a child, my grandfather and I had always been close. He would take me fishing, baited my hook, and let me chatter on. That, of course, scared away the fish but he didn't seem to mind very much. He showed me how to "dip" for minnies. Using a minnow net and a flour paste mixture, he taught me how to apply it. He always caught the crawfish so they wouldn't pitch my fingers. I was the one he would give a bite of turkey or ham to on the holidays. He would grumble at everyone else to stay out of the kitchen while he was carving. A lot of people thought he was gruff and a little bit mean. But I would laugh at him when he started his grouching. When he became seriously ill from complications of diabetes, I would push him up and down the hospital corridors in his wheelchair. The day he died was a sad day in my young life. I was eleven.

As I grew older, married, divorced, and married again, I often thought of my grandfather. I wasn't surprised, looking back on this incident in hindsight, when the impossible became the possible.

It began during an uneasy day that led into an even edgier night. My husband, at the time, had been having some severe mental problems. He had been treated at a mental clinic and released about three weeks prior. My family was concerned for my personal safety. I had already given my father all the guns and anything I thought would be dangerous. Although my husband was on medication, his paranoia was still evident. He had told me men in black cars were following him. He said his mail was being read by a special ultraviolet light before being delivered. He had been muttering under his breath, peering out the window, and just acting strangely.

Earlier that day when he was at an appointment, I had found an odd wire going up the wall concealed in a crack. It led from the telephone, up the wall, and across the ceiling tiles. Up in the tiles was a small tape recorder that was hooked up to the phone. There was a pile of tapes beside it. He had been recording all phone conversations coming in and out of our home. I had no idea how long it had been going on. Feeling nervous, I put the ceiling tile back in place. When he came home, I didn't mention it to him because I didn't know what reaction I would get.

As night fell, he was restless, making disjointed statements and becoming agitated. I had finally gotten him to take his medication. He was resting on the couch with his eyes closed. Just before he drifted off he looked me straight in the eye. He had a wild look in his eye as he told me "they" would never take him alive… or me either. He had plans to prevent it. Then he rolled over and went to sleep.

I went into the bedroom and locked the door. I was weary to the bone. Emotionally and physically exhausted, I felt at the end of my resources. Now I wasn't just uneasy but I was afraid too. I undressed, letting the clothes lay where they fell, and turned out the light. I pulled the curtains back so the streetlight would shine into the room. I couldn't face being alone in the dark. The light from the streetlight streamed in, casting light in the corners of the room. I climbed wearily into bed.

After turning and tossing, I fell into a restless sleep. I was asleep for some time when I woke up to my name being called. "Linda, Linda, wake up!" I could hear my husband snoring in the other room so I knew it wasn't him.

At first I couldn't see anything. Peering warily, I looked down toward the bottom of the bed near the dresser. At the foot of the bed was a strange, dark smoky fog. It was the height of a person but the shape was ill-defined. It had a swirling movement within the shape, as if the smoky fog were whirling inside. Little flecks of silver sparkles reflected among the whirls. The dresser could be seen faintly through it. From this apparition was where the voice was coming from. I heard the haunting, familiar voice again.

"Linda, you know what he is capable of. You know what he can do. You have to leave!"

I was, at this point, flat up against the headboard. Definitely wide-awake. My heart was pounding and I broke out in a cold sweat, chills running up and down my spine. The voice repeated again with more force, almost commanding.

"Linda, you know what he is capable of. You have to leave!"

Suddenly I realized, with a sudden jolt, that I was hearing the voice of my beloved grandfather. I had not heard his voice for twenty years! He came to warn me I was in danger. As I watched in amazement and disbelief, the gray fog slowly swirled and dissolved. The outline of the dresser could be seen clearly again. My husband was still snoring in the other room; what I saw and heard did not affect him. I turned on the light and lay awake, trying to figure what I was going to do.

The next morning when my husband left for awhile, I went down the road and called my parents from a pay phone. I told them about my husband's instability, the phone tapping, and finally about the specter visit. My father informed me I was moving out of there and fast. I went that day and found an apartment. I knew my husband had appointments for the following day, so we made plans to move me then. I slept there one more night with the door locked and one eye open.

When my husband left the next day, I called my family. They showed up in a half hour. They had me packed and out the door in an hour and a half. My father had informed the police there might be a problem. They were familiar with my husband from previous dealings and sent an officer out to make sure there weren't going to be any incidents. After moving out I filed for divorce.

My husband committed himself to a state institution for six months. He admitted to me afterward that he had planned on doing away with me, the dog, and himself within the next couple of days.

Was it really my grandfather who warned me to leave? I believe that he came back through from the other side. He did whatever he needed to do to reach me. He knew what was going to happen and prevented it. I believe that now and I always will.

Linda Lee Ruzicka is fifty years old, happily married, with a fourteen-year old daughter. She lives in the mountains of Western Pennsylvania with her family, three dogs, and a cat. Linda works at home writing poetry and short stories. She is also working on a children's book.

She is currently involved in finishing up a two-year course in writing for children. She has completed a course on personal experience and started a course in adult writing.

Seven of Linda's poems have been published in *The Dark Krypt*. She has had five poems published in *Twilight Times* with one upcoming in the December issue. Linda also has a poem in the June Cotner anthology series *Housewarming* (published in May 2004) with acceptance of two other poems in forthcoming books. Another poem appeared in the Winter 2004 issue of *Fables*.

Lingering Love

by Nancy Jackson

It was a distinct smell that lingered in my room, long after I turned off the bedside lamp. I lay there, grieving my beloved grandfather, the only one who had shown me complete love and kindness. I tried to place the scent, sweet and jam-like. Then it came to me—fresh strawberries! I instantly jumped out of bed and turned on the light. My heart pounded like an ancient tribal drum as I stared at the now special spot in my room. A light hazy figure stood there, looking like a patch of mist or fog. I couldn't make out any features, but it was the smell that let me know who was there. Grandpa.

My grandfather took care of me on the weekends during summer vacation. Both my parents worked and I begged to not be cast off from one sitter to the next like so many of my friends. To my excitement, they gave in and I haven't ever experienced a summer quite like that again. I grew to cherish the bond this older man and I shared from day one. Each and every weekend we tended to his beautiful fruit and vegetable garden, but it was his strawberries that sealed the deal. He had to have grown the largest, juiciest strawberries I had ever seen in my whole seven years of life. Entrusting me with the tin watering can, I made several journeys back and forth from the rusted faucet in the kitchen, carefully hydrating those sweet treats. He called me his strawberry shortcake and nothing could have erased the smile from my face.

Late afternoons we lounged along the porch, indulging in large bowls of vanilla ice cream topped with mounds of fresh strawberries. Afterward we would sit together and talk until he fell asleep. In those precious moments I listened to his breathing calm me like a gentle wind. Rarely did I fall asleep; I was much too fascinated by the movements his face would make as he dreamt.

Coming home Mom would fuss over my berry juice stained shirts, but I didn't care; it was something of Grandpa that I brought home with me. We became best friends and confidants. There wasn't a thing I did that he didn't praise me for. My confidence soared as our relationship grew. I never wanted our special time to end.

I dreaded the last weekend with him before my return to school. While my family and I still visited Grandpa during the school year, it was never the same. With my parents around we couldn't have our secret talks or laugh over all our inside jokes. After that, my next few summers were spent at camp and soon he grew sick and had a stroke, leaving his memory somewhere behind. It angered me that he was placed in a nursing home, deemed too weak to care for himself. It didn't sound right to me—he was the strongest man I knew!

My last visit with him at the age of ten years left me in tears, and I told myself I couldn't see him again because it hurt too much. He didn't even know who I was anymore! His face was black, uncomprehending, as I clumsily embraced his now wheel-chair-bound body. My heart didn't want to accept that this was how he would be from now on. I hoped somewhere inside there was a small part of me in his mind that would never go away. I gave him a silent farewell and from then on made up excuses to keep my distance.

Two years later, we received the call that my grandfather had passed away. Built-up pain and anger formed cascades of tears that drenched my face, hair, and the collar of my shirt. I threw myself upon my bed and wept for hours until I fell asleep. Visions plagued my mind as I was somewhere between sleep and waking up. The clock blinked one in the morning but the aroma permeated my small room, creating a comforting safe haven. I stared at that hazy figure, picturing my grandfather's face, etching the wrinkled lines around his eyes, remembering his bright blue eyes that twinkled when he smiled. I fell to my knees and bowed my head, wanting to hide my shame for not being with him in his last hours.

Somehow he must have known this and came to me, allowing me to be with him one last time. Softly, so my parents would not hear, I confessed all my feelings, begging forgiveness, sharing with him what I had been keeping to myself. I told him he had forgotten me, and how it had hurt worse than a paper cut ever could. It had broken my heart.

For a flash of a moment I could clearly make out his face, and it was the same eyes and smile that I saw every weekend of that glorious summer. He even had the little tufts of hair sticking out from his ears. I smiled back, feeling freedom inside from having released all of my hidden pain. The hair on my body stood straight up but not out of fear. It was the most calming, soothing sensation I had ever felt. Warmth spread through the room, a gift of love from him to me. I didn't dare look away, afraid to miss a single expression. He leaned forward and placed a kiss upon my forehead. While I only felt light pressure, it filled me with beautiful thoughts. Suddenly I could see as if looking through a window, into his garden, the garden he would be attending to in his afterlife. Rows and rows of strawberries plastered the ground and I knew he would be happy where he was going, for he loved gardening; it was his passion. I was so blessed to have shared that passion with him. Over and over I expressed how much he meant to me and how much I loved him. I told him that he had been an inspiration to me and a strong role model. I let him know he could never be replaced and that I wished him well in the place he was headed. I asked him to not forget me and to visit whenever he wanted. With a nod of his head, he vanished. A rush of emotions filled my insides. I hated to see him go, but I knew deep down inside that he would always be with me.

I have never seen his hazy shape again, but every now and then, when I feel down or am ready to give up, the delicious smell fills my senses and lets me know I am never alone. Our love and companionship lingers on, as does the scent of strawberries.

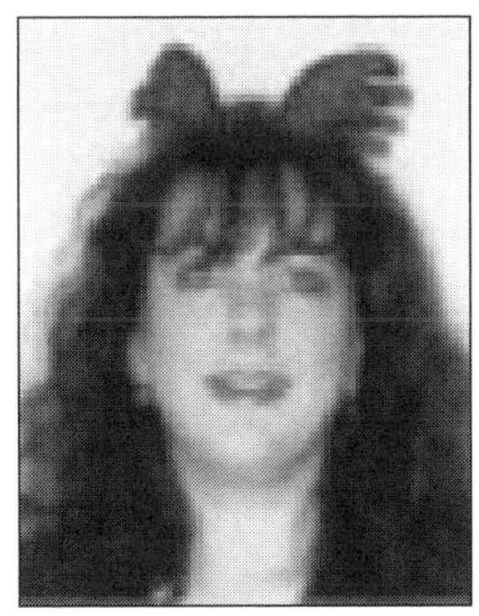

Nancy Jackson is a full-time writer, editor, book reviewer, partner, and mother. Her work can be seen online, in magazines, and in several anthologies. To find out more, please check out her web site at http://www.nancyajackson.com.

Kati and the Dolphins

by Renie Burghardt

When I was fourteen and Kati was fifteen, both our families received the news we had been waiting for. We were going to America!

For destitute Hungarian refugees who had been living in a refugee camp for the past four years, this was wonderful news. It was our chance at a new life in a new country. What was even more wonderful was that Kati and I, who were best friends, were going to America at the same time.

In September 1951, we boarded the *General M.B. Stewart* with hundreds of other hopeful refugees. Once on board, we streamed to our assigned quarters on the ship—women and children separated from the men and older boys. Kati and I would be sleeping next to each other in upper bunks with our mothers directly below us.

When the ship finally pulled out to sea, we gathered on the deck. It was a poignant moment, especially for the adults, who realized sadly that they wouldn't be seeing their old homeland again.

"But we are on our way to America, the land of the free and the brave," Kati declared joyously, echoing my own sentiment. She and I embraced this new adventure with much hope in our hearts, putting the hardships World War II had dealt us behind.

Of course, Kati and I soon began to explore the ship. We ate together in the massive dining hall and played together in the

208

huge recreation room on the ship. Meanwhile, both her parents and mine spent most of their time in bed, suffering from seasickness.

By the second day on the ship, Kati and I had even made a friend. He was a young American who worked in the galley and brought us extra treats on his breaks while telling us all about life in the United States. Of course, I realized that Dave's interest in us was due to Kati's good looks. She had long, curly black hair framing her oval face and her body was already that of a young woman's, while my body was still in limbo, like my braided locks. However, Dave's attention was fun and we looked forward to his visits.

On the third day of our voyage as Kati and I sat in the recreation room leafing through a book, Dave rushed in and motioned to us.

"Come on, girls. I want to show you something," he said excitedly.

We jumped up and followed him to the deck.

"Look! Dolphins!" Dave said, pointing out on the Atlantic.

"Oh… they are beautiful!" Kati cried breathlessly. The playful creatures enchanted me as well. We counted six of them, diving and carrying on out there in the great waves. It was a wonderful spectacle.

"Listen! They are talking to us," Kati then said, leaning so far down on the railing that she frightened me. I pulled at her jacket and cautioned, "Be careful or you will fall in the water."

"Oh, I wouldn't mind that in the least," Kati said with a laugh. "They are calling me. It would be wonderful to join them and ride the waves on their backs."

"It would not be wonderful for you. You are not a dolphin, so you wouldn't survive down there," Dave said seriously. Kati gave him a strange look, and then she walked away from us.

After that, Kati became obsessed with the dolphins. She looked for them and talked about them day and night, and I, not knowing how to handle her new obsession, grew more and more concerned about her. Even when there weren't any dolphins out there, Kati claimed she could hear them calling her, and nothing Dave and I said, persuaded her that it wasn't so. Her obsession frightened me.

On the sixth day of our ten-day journey, Kati suddenly became very ill. Her mother, thinking she was seasick, made her stay in her bunk all that day. Of course, I kept her company.

"Do you feel sick to your stomach?" I asked her several times.

"Maybe a little," she replied. "I'll be all right by tomorrow."

That night, as I lay on my sleeping bunk across from Kati, thinking she was asleep, I suddenly heard her moan. The she whispered, "Yes, I'm coming. I'm coming."

"Kati, who are you talking to?" I asked, sitting up. But instead of a reply, I heard her soft, lilting laughter. Kati was in her bunk, but her laughter was floating above me, moving across the entire area before disappearing into the night. I sat up and called out loudly, "Kati! Kati! Are you all right?"

By this time both Kati's mother and my mother woke up and got out of their bunks to see what the problem was.

"Kati is gone," I wailed, tears streaming down my cheeks. "She went to join the dolphins."

"What do you mean she is gone? She is lying right there, in her bunk," my baffled mother said, while Kati's mother climbed up and shook her daughter.

"Oh my God! She is dead! Oh my God!" Kati's mother screamed, waking everyone up. The ship's doctor was summoned. But it was too late. They took Kati away.

The doctor said she had pneumonia. The kind that strikes like a blitz. Her mother, blaming herself for Kati's death, became so depressed that she would not utter another word for the rest of the journey. I was pretty depressed myself.

Two days before we arrived in New York harbor, I was up on the deck, watching the waves lapping at the ship. Suddenly, several dolphins appeared and began carrying on with their usual antics. But I didn't call down to them as before. I just stood there and watched them silently. Then I heard something. "Whee, this is wonderful." It was Kati's voice. There was no doubt about it.

"You hear it too, don't you?" A voice behind me said, startling me. It was Dave. We kept standing there in silence, listening to the lilting laughter below. Finally, the dolphins dove under and disappeared.

"Good bye, Kati," I shouted after them. "I will miss you. I will never forget you."

Of course, our arrival in New York was a somber occasion for Kati's parents. While other people were rejoicing to be there to start new lives in a new country, they had to think about burying their daughter in this new land. My heart ached for them. I longed to tell them not to be sad, to tell them Kati's spirit was happy among the dolphins, but I knew they wouldn't believe me. Instead, I gave them both a long hug, and then walked away in silence. But the truth would be tucked into my heart for eternity.

Renie Burghardt is a freelance writer who was born in Hungary. Her work has been published in a number of books—including *Chicken Soup*, *Chocolate for Women*, *Cup of Comfort*, and *Guideposts*—and magazines such as *Mature Living*, *Missouri Life*, *Midwest Living*, and *Angels on Earth*.

She lives in the country and loves nature, animals, gardening, reading, hiking, jet skiing on the river, and spending time with family and friends.

An Encounter with Grandpa

by Tennille Langille

I was devastated when my grandpa died. My grandfather on my father's side had passed away before I was born, so my grandpa was the only one I knew.

My grandpa owned a general contracting business. He was a big, strong man on the outside and full of love on the inside. He had served in World War II and was a Pearl Harbor survivor. He had also built the house I grew up in that was nestled in the mountains of San Diego County, California.

After he retired, my grandpa had so much time on his hands that he didn't know what to do with himself. He found that he enjoyed putting together complicated jigsaw puzzles and doing odd jobs around the house. However, his body was conditioned to doing strenuous physical work and his burly frame began withering away. He began to show his age. It was a longtime family joke that Grandpa was forgetful. A while after his retirement, he was diagnosed with dementia, a disease with symptoms similar to Alzheimer's. At first, he didn't seem changed by the disease. But after a few years, we all began to see a difference. Grandpa's forgetfulness soon surpassed the inconvenience of misplaced keys or a forgotten wallet. He would forget that he had put toast in the toaster and set off the smoke alarm. He would forget to close the door and the cat would run away. He would get up in the middle of the night and not remember where he was. Day by day, things mounted up and my grandmother finally coaxed him into being entertained all day in front of the television in his brown armchair. His health deteriorated quickly, and before I knew it, I was answering the phone to hear my mother telling me that Grandpa had died.

In the days following my grandpa's death, I helped my mother and grandmother arrange his memorial service and cremation. We spent the days thumbing through photo albums to find pictures for his service. I spent my evenings writing a poem for him. I read it to my grandmother after its completion and she asked me to read it at his memorial service.

On the day of the memorial service, I was much more emotional than I had prepared myself for. I didn't think I would be able to get through the reading, but somehow I did. I had to stop after each line and catch my breath and clear my quavering voice. I listened to countless friends and relatives share their special stories about him. I began to feel regretful that his last days were so full of suffering, and that I, along with the rest of the family, had not been as compassionate and understanding of his condition as we should have been. His forgetfulness and dependency on all of us for everything was tiring and I often found myself avoiding him so that I didn't have to deal with it. Partly it was out of selfishness, but part of it was that it was too hard to see my big, strong grandpa in such a state of confusion and weakness.

I fell asleep on the couch that night. I lived in a two-story townhouse at the time. The staircase was fashioned in two parts: a first series of steps, a landing, then the second series of steps went up diagonally from the first. The couch was positioned so that you could see the first series of stairs and the landing. I awoke in the middle of the night and had an eerie feeling that someone was watching me. I rolled over and waited for my eyes to adjust to the dark. I saw someone standing on the landing. I was sure it was my husband coming downstairs to see why I wasn't in bed yet. As I focused in on the figure, I realized it was not my husband. I thought someone had broken into our house. I looked over at the front door, but it was still closed and locked. No one could have gotten through the front door without me knowing it, as I was twenty feet away. I looked to my right and saw that the back door was still locked and the curtains were drawn. I began to feel panicky that I couldn't get upstairs to my husband without passing by the intruder first.

I asked, "What do you want?" The stranger did not answer. Why was he just standing there? I pulled myself up to a sitting position and was finally able to see the features of the stranger's face. I felt the blood drain from my face. It was my grandfather. I felt afraid at first, as I had never had an encounter with a ghost, and had never really wanted to. I tried to swallow and couldn't. I tried to speak and couldn't. I finally just sat there and studied his appearance. He didn't look like he did in his last years. He was young again, maybe in his mid-twenties. He was wearing his Army uniform and hat and looked just like the photograph I had displayed of him when he was stationed in the Pacific in the 1940s. He looked so serious and was just staring back at me.

Although I felt foolish doing it, I remember pinching myself to see if I was dreaming. I wasn't. I didn't like how cross he looked. I thought perhaps he was angry with me for avoiding him during his last days or because I wasn't as kind as I should have been. I finally found my voice and said softly, "Grandpa?" The stern expression relaxed and my grandfather's signature ear-to-ear smile broke out over his face. As his lips parted, I saw the gap between his front teeth, and I knew for certain that it was my grandpa.

When I got up off the couch and started for the stairs, he vanished. As quickly as he had arrived, he was gone. I'm not sure why he looked so uptight in those first few moments, but it almost seemed like he wasn't sure where he was. He had only been to my house once before and maybe he wasn't sure if he had come to the right one. As soon as I spoke to him, he had relaxed and given me that big smile.

I told my family about my experience the next day. Everyone was touched that I had been able to see him and that he looked well. I'm not sure why he came back, but I am happy that he did. I felt so much better knowing he was no longer suffering and that he was happy. I felt especially comforted knowing that he's still around and watching over us. I always thought if I ever saw a ghost it would be a frightening experience. I changed my mind after seeing my grandfather in spiritual form. It was a very calming and reassuring feeling, knowing that someone you loved mortally is watching over you spiritually. I hope he comes to see me again someday.

Tennille Langille was born and raised in Southern California. She discovered her love for writing at a young age and spent much of her time reading and writing stories. Her twelfth-grade English literature teacher, impressed with her writing skills, nominated her for inclusion in *Who's Who Among American High School Students* (she appeared in the 1996 edition). She received her first publication credit at age nineteen for a poem she submitted to a poetry contest. Upon her marriage in 2002, she relocated to Honolulu, Hawaii. She currently works for the State of Hawaii and also does freelance writing. She recently completed the freelance writing program offered by Thompson's

Education Direct and is currently taking courses through the Institute of Children's Literature and the American Writers & Artists Institute. She plans to turn her freelance writing into a full-time career.

White Birds

by Heidi McDonald

B y the time Harry died, he weighed 98 pounds, had no hair or teeth left, ate and eliminated through tubes, and was a legless amputee in a Mexican AIDS ward. Had I seen him this way, it would have broken my heart.

Harry had AIDS for as long as I had known him. In 1986, he visited the church where my mother was the associate pastor. In the course of her pastoral calls to visitors, it was revealed that Harry (a boisterous, red-headed, bearded man with a delicious tenor singing voice, who was as comfortable in cowboy boots as he was in size 11 ladies' high-heeled shoes) had been disowned by his Texan Baptist family upon the realization that he was gay and had AIDS.

Our family at that time was a mother and two-daughter unit, recently having separated the father part from its ranks. It seemed to make sense—our family wasn't whole anymore, and Harry had been thrown away by his family. We decided to adopt him. He became my brother.

There are many world views about AIDS and about the nature of homosexuals. Mostly because of knowing Harry, I can't hate people because they were born "different." I'm quite sure, in fact, that Harry agonized greatly upon realizing he was gay because he knew what that would mean in terms of his life and his family. In the eyes of many, he was a sinner. But in my eyes, he's someone who lived and died honestly and was a human being as real as anyone.

It was certainly an experience to have a brother who'd borrow earrings from you or evaluate your boyfriends for their respective level of attractiveness. It was certainly handy to have someone who could tinker with your car or take you places you were too embarrassed to go with your mom. It was certainly hilarious to see him dress up as Tammy Faye Bakker or a member of the Village People on Halloween… or to watch him egg the rest of the family into balancing spoons on our noses at Thanksgiving dinner. It was certainly annoying to have him tell outrageous tales in front of your friends or be kissing on the front porch, only to have Harry flip the porch lights on and holler, "Inside, now, Babygirl! Go, go, go, go!" It was certainly poignant to hear him sing *O Holy Night* every Christmas Eve, wondering how many more times we'd get to hear it.

We expected Harry to die, because that's what happens to people who have AIDS. We even talked at length about how he felt about dying, what he thought he'd find after he died, and how he wanted us to handle his funeral. One Saturday in the fall, seated on the same antique pink couch he'd chastised me for kissing my boyfriend on, we talked about death.

"When you die, will you try to send me something, like a sign, so we know you're OK and happy and still around?" I asked.

"Babygirl, I'll never be outta your hair," he drawled, rolling his eyes.

"OK, so what will you send me? A drag queen?" I laughed, playfully batting him on the arm.

"No," he said thoughtfully, looking into the sky with pause. We saw a dove go winging over the house, perhaps on its way south for the upcoming winter. "There," he said. "That. A white bird. Whenever you see a white bird go past at an unusual place or at an unusual time, that'll be me."

We sat there, holding hands and watching the bird disappear into the distance. Neither of us wanted to say anything, it seemed, because he was slipping away into the distance just like the bird, and we somehow thought not talking about it would delay his exit from the world and from a perfect moment like that one. He soon left our midst to participate in experimental treatments in Mexico. Knowing he was deteriorating, he didn't want to burden or upset us with the end of his life, which came one afternoon while he was propped in front of a television set with a forbidden cigarette dangling from his mouth.

When the news of his death came one July afternoon in 1993, no matter how prepared I thought was, I was devastated. We had a memorial service at the church with his picture but with no urn. His ashes had somehow disappeared in the mail. If he were any other person, we would have investigated the matter until it was resolved, but to a free spirit like Harry's, the disappearance of his ashes made a certain amount of sense, like that white bird disappearing into the distance that long-ago autumn day.

I spent months looking for white birds but never saw any. So many times I needed Harry. I needed his advice, wanted him around to talk to, but he was gone. In hope, I'd turn my face up to the sky. But I never saw a white bird and soon I stopped looking for them. I went on with my life as people must when they lose someone special, putting myself through school as a professional musician. My mother went on to write a book about how Harry had changed her mind about gay people and people with AIDS, and spent much of her time traveling and lecturing. My sister moved to Columbus and began her adulthood. When Harry went, our family scattered as easily as birds—or the mysterious missing ashes.

Two years later, having dropped out of college due to an unexpected pregnancy, I welcomed my baby daughter Annie in April 1995. In fact, she came on April 15, and my taxes were late that year. When we were released from the hospital two days later, I was sore, tired, and feeling overwhelmed at having gone from an uncomfortably large woman to the sole caretaker of a crying infant within a day's space. We still have the picture of Annie and me being rolled out of Magee Hospital in a wheelchair. The photo didn't capture the expression on my face when I looked directly across the parking lot and saw a single white pigeon perched atop the hospital marquee. This could have been any bird, on any day, but I knew it had to be Harry, because it was also snowing that day and there were no other birds around. As I cried on the way home, Annie's father said something about my hormone levels.

I also cried the first time I ever heard myself call Annie "Babygirl." I hadn't planned on doing so—it just slipped out. I made a conscious decision to teach my children about their Uncle Harry, while knowing how much he might have loved them. My son Simon was born two years later, and about a year after that, the three of us made a night escape to the safety of my mother's house. Driving from the home the kids and I shared with their father in the panhandle of West Virginia, I was crying so hard I could barely see the road. I was scared, wondering how I'd handle single parenthood. I was sad, grieving for a marriage I'd begun with the best of intentions. I decided to pull over for a minute and finish crying before I continued.

Once I had regained enough composure to continue driving, I saw what I thought was a white bird fly directly over my car. It happened very quickly. I turned around to see whether my kids had seen it too, but instantly remembered that it was the middle of the night and both kids were asleep. I continued on the road toward Pittsburgh, wondering whether I'd actually seen one of

Harry's white birds or whether my mind was playing tricks on me. At the exact moment I was wondering this, I passed an outdoor billboard for a Christian station, which had a white dove on it. I said out loud, "Coincidence."

Then, defiantly, I turned on the radio for the rest of my drive—"Take It Easy" by the Eagles was playing. Eagles, of course, are birds. And The Eagles, the musicians, are from Texas just as Harry was from Texas. I couldn't dismiss it anymore. I laughed harder than I'd remember laughing in a long time. Harry was there, for sure. I heard a sleepy child shift in the back seat, my Babygirl, and felt sure everything would somehow turn out all right.

One day about a year later, I was stopped in rush-hour traffic when an old friend from high school pulled up beside me in a nearby car. On the day I married him in 2001, our new family stood together, freshly married and deliciously happy, on the front stairs of the hall. I looked across to the adjacent park and saw a flock of white birds flying up into the sky. It sounds like it was too good to be true, and at the time, it felt that way.

I have since come to realize that whenever I have a life-altering moment, my brother will be there, reminding me that he still loves and watches over his Babygirl. It was only when I stopped looking for the white birds and started living my life that I was able to see "a white bird go past at an unusual place or at an unusual time." In the meantime, it's up to me and my family to make sure Harry is never forgotten. Annie and Simon are pretty good at putting spoons on their noses at holiday time, as Harry's picture beams down at us from the mantel.

Writer, musician, politician, and activist Heidi McDonald (www.heidiwrites.com) began writing in the fourth grade and lives in Edgewood, Pennsylvania, with her husband, three children, and a beagle. In 2000 her copywriting was recognized with a Silver Microphone Award; in 2002, one of her short stories was a winning entry in a worldwide contest sponsored by actor Rutger Hauer; in 2003, she was elected to her local borough council, where she currently serves; and in 2004, Heidi was honored with a Golden Quill Award from the Press Club of Western Pennsylvania for her cover story in *Pittsburgh City Paper* about the complexities of obesity. Musically, she was honored in 2002 with an opportunity to perform onstage with her favorite musician, Neil Finn; their performance received mention on MTV.

Published in many regional publications and on the Internet, Heidi has served as a fiction juror for *ELLE* magazine, and a judge in the flash fiction contest at Whim's Place online. She is the Family Fun editor for Garden and Hearth Online and served as a humor editor and site contributor for IGN. Her favorite types of writing are humor and op-ed, and she is currently working on a screenplay. Interspersed in the family mayhem are her hobbies, which include reading, cooking, and quilting, as well as helping each of her kids turn in the most creative homework assignments in the whole class. Great-grandniece of 1930s movie star Zelma O'Neal, Heidi prides herself on being a movie buff with a particular fondness for the Oscars.

Grandma Linnie's Last Visit

by Anne Culbreath Watkins

My Grandma Linnie was an extraordinary woman who was known for sleeping with a set of brass knuckles underneath her pillow, right alongside a pistol and a wickedly sharp butcher knife. However eccentric that may sound, she had a good reason for her bizarre behavior. Widowed at a young age with three little boys, she was their sole protector and caretaker. Besides that, she faced extreme challenges that would daunt a lesser person—Grandma Linnie was also profoundly deaf.

In the early 1900s, people sometimes suffered terrible complications from diseases that are easily treated or prevented these days. My paternal grandmother was one of those people. Robbed of her hearing by an illness when she was sixteen years old, she nevertheless spoke well, having learned speech patterns and inflections before her illness. Her speech didn't have the flat, tonal sounds usually associated with the deaf, and the only words that gave her any trouble were words she hadn't learned before going deaf. She had a soft, Southern accent, and I never tired of listening to her sweet voice.

Grandma Linnie taught me sign language when I was very small, and we also used family-specific hand gestures to communicate. Since she was a skilled lip reader, too, I often yelled questions at her when we were in public. People outside the family gave me strange looks when they saw me shouting at the old lady who smiled and nodded at this screeching child gesticulating madly before her. I didn't care; Grandma Linnie understood what I meant.

I loved to visit her house, and walks to the local general store were the high points of my days because I knew that Grandma would let me have all the candy and soda I wanted. She also fixed me banana sandwiches, let me page through her movie star and gossip magazines, and told me horrifying ghost stories—stories she swore were true—that made my hair stand on end. And to my fascination, every night she sliced up a lemon and ate it as she slowly sipped a cup of warm water fizzing with an antacid tablet. Well known for being the family hypochondriac, this was one of Grandma's health tonics, and I wanted to try it, too. One taste was all it took to convince me to let her enjoy her nightly ritual in peace.

My father was one of Grandma Linnie's oldest three sons, and she had two more boys from her second marriage. Out of all these sons, Grandma gained lots of grandchildren, and I fell somewhere in the middle of the group. My boy cousins by far outnumbered the girls, and as we all grew up and ventured out into the world, Grandma made no secret of the fact that she expected us all to get married and provide her with lots of great-grandchildren—especially female great-grandchildren.

When I got married, she immediately began asking when I planned to have a baby. It took two years, but finally I was delighted to discover that I was expecting. And when I gave birth to my little baby girl, I named her Laura Lynn, after Grandma.

One night, while the house was quiet and empty, I took advantage of the time and put myself and my brand-new daughter down for some much needed rest. While Laura snoozed peacefully in her bassinet near me, I dozed off, trying to ignore the snoring coming from my husband's side of the bed.

I had always been a light sleeper, but seemed even more so since the baby was born, and it didn't take much to wake me. A slight movement in the darkened bedroom sent my eyes flying open, and I turned toward the crib. To my surprise and pleasure, Grandma Linnie was standing quietly beside the bassinet. She gathered the baby up without waking her, and then cradled the precious bundle gently in her arms.

"She's so purty," she said in her soft Southern accent. Waves of love as tangible and real as a cozy blanket enfolded me.

"Thank you," I replied, smiling as Grandma Linnie admired the baby girl she had waited so long for. She brushed her lips against Laura's forehead and smoothed back the hair from her tiny face.

I sat up in bed, wrapped my arms around my knees, and happily chatted with Grandma about the baby for several moments. Then a rustling to my left caught my attention and I noticed the other visitors lingering in the darkness of the hallway. "Who are they?" I asked. Grandma Linnie glanced over her shoulder and smiled. "Some friends of mine," she said. "We can't stay long, but they wanted to see the baby, too."

The shadowy figures, two men and a woman, stirred and whispered. Though their faces were obscured by the dimness, vibes of happiness radiated from them. Then one of them beckoned to Grandma. She nodded a response and cuddled my daughter a few more minutes before snuggling the baby back into the bassinet. "She sure is purty," Grandma repeated.

"Thank you," I said. "I love you, Grandma."

"I love you, too, honey," she said. She bent to kiss Laura on the cheek once more. Then, giving me one last smile, she left the room. Laura sighed a sleepy murmur of contentment, and I drifted back to sleep, basking in the warmth of Grandma Linnie's love.

The next morning, my husband asked, "Who were you talking to last night?"

"Why?" I wanted to know. "Did it bother you?"

"No," he replied. "It just sounded like you were having a long conversation with somebody. I fell back asleep before you were done."

"Sorry," I said with a shrug. "Didn't mean to wake you up." I grinned quietly to myself as I thought of the night before, and in the days that followed the sweetness of Grandma's visit remained wrapped around my heart and soul like a fluffy down comforter. And while it's been twenty-four years since that special night, those wonderful, warm feelings still touch me whenever I think about it. But there is also a sense of wonder connected to that long-ago visit. You see, Grandma Linnie died more than a year before my daughter, her namesake, was born.

Anne Culbreath Watkins is the author of *The Conure Handbook* (Barron's Educational Series, Inc.). A full-time freelance writer/photographer, her work has appeared in numerous print publications such as *Angels on Earth*, *Bird Talk*, *Companion Parrot Quarterly*, *Fate*, *Pet Age*, and *Whispers from Heaven*, as well as in more than two dozen anthologies. Anne and her banjo-player husband, Allen, live in Alabama where they love to spoil their grandchildren, Bailey, Chelsea, and Tyler. Visit her online at http://www.geocities.com/anne_ c _watkins.

Dad's Room

by Christina Kiplinger-Johns

I was thirty-eight years old when I found my father dead. I don't think it's ever a good time for a child to find a parent dead. Especially if the child has been living with the parent, and taking care of the parent, and finally having a grown-up relationship with the parent! No, I don't think it's ever a good time to find a parent dead. As a matter of fact, I think it's bad news.

At least the day Dad died was sunny and bright.

April and the flowers were blooming all over the place.

On this particular day, my father and I had talked about installing a small gravel drive in front of the seven-room brick home we lived in. It was becoming a nuisance to be without street parking when nurses came to visit Dad. Though Dad was legally blind and suffering from the effects of having long-term diabetes and not taking care of himself, he was trying to make the best of his illness.

"Of course we need a place for all of these pretty little nurses to park," He smiled when we had talked earlier that day. My dad was a charmer with the ladies. "I like that one, Chris. What was her name? The redhead?"

"Linda."

"Ah, yeah... Linda," Dad said with a twinkle in his eye. "You know, if I weren't married, Linda would have a choice to make!"

"And it would be a tough choice too, Dad." I smiled.

228

Dad had been married to Callie for the fifteen years that he and Mom had been divorced. We were lucky that all people involved could remain friends. Mom and Dad had known each other since elementary school, and I think that was a lot of the reason the two got along after the divorce. They had known each other forever. Dad and I had been alone in this house for about a month. Callie had been put in a nursing home by the state, under loud protest from Dad. Callie suffered from advanced Alzheimer's and needed daily nursing care. Though she was away, and very ill, Dad remained constant to her.

"How are you feeling today, Dad?" I had a thought in mind.

"I feel pretty good," Dad said, "I probably feel better than I have felt in the last month."

"Great," I said as I gathered my purse and light jacket. "Maybe we'll go see Callie when I get back."

"That sounds fine," Dad said as he became distracted by the home-shopping network. He often bought gifts for family members from television. With the ways of the modern world and uncaring people, I felt much better having Dad order from TV than taking him to the mall. Dad agreed.

By the time I finally made it to Fame Hair, it was about 6 p.m. The laughing and joking was a refreshing change from the somber conditions at home. My haircut was completed in twenty minutes and I was on my way to take Dad to see Callie.

When I parked in the side drive of the house, our cat, Boots, ran up to me and encircled my legs in a motion that seemed to mean, "Hello, I'm glad to see you." Boots enjoyed being out in the neighborhood during the warm days. He was known by neighbors as one of the best chipmunk catchers around, and many family jokes centered on the cat and his antics.

Boots didn't care. His only problem, of late, was with Toby, the small Yorkshire terrier I had brought home to keep Dad company. Boots and Toby did not get along at all.

As we stood at that door, the climate had changed. Toby licked Boots in the face, and for some odd reason, the cat didn't move away as he usually did. The cat seemed to wait for his welcome.

"Wait until I tell your dad what you have been doing, Toby!" I scolded the pup. "HE is really going to get a good laugh!"

Opening the door, I noticed a calm had set into the house. It seemed as if everything was still. Making my way into the bedroom to see if Dad was resting on the bed, I hurriedly approached his reclining form.

"Dad," I excitedly said. "You'll never believe what Toby did!"

Dad was very still. Too still. When I looked closely at his face, it was an ashen gray. My Dad was dead.

The flurry of excitement following that discovery is one that only other people who have experienced it can understand. Relatives were ringing the phone off the hook. Calls were made to the undertaker, after the police had taken Dad to the hospital for confirmation of death. Things were all in a forward motion.

My twenty five-year-old daughter came from a nearby town to assist me in the preparations. I was very glad to have someone at my side who I knew could be counted on and trusted. My daughter would be very helpful.

Before going to bed that first night, my daughter and I sat at the table in the kitchen my father had loved. On a near wall, a normal enough looking wall clock, its face full of fruit decorations, rested on the wall.

"Did you ever figure out why Grandpa liked that clock so much?" My daughter asked.

"No," I said and smiled my first smile since my discovery.

"It's OK, I guess," Karen mused. "But I wouldn't hang it in my kitchen!"

At the very second that sentence left my daughter's mouth, a nearby CD player blasted my father's most loved recording by The Miami Sound Machine. Staring at the machine, I managed a half smile and turned it off.

"How did that turn on?" my daughter asked.

"I don't know, but we have a busy day tomorrow—I think we need to go to bed now."

That's exactly what we did.

I woke up from a black dreamless sleep to my daughter calling for me.

"Mom," Karen yelled into the room. "Mom, the funeral home is on the phone for you."

That's how my entire day went. Calls and visits to the funeral home, more calls from relatives and friends wishing me well filled the day, and Karen and I ordered out for dinner.

"Hey, Mom," Karen said over the dinner table. "Why did Callie's daughter tell you that you have to move out of here?"

"Well, because Callie is in a nursing home and they plan to sell the house."

"Bet Grandpa didn't know about that! Didn't he want you to have this place?"

"Well," I began the yarn. "For one thing, the deed was a joint ownership. That means that it went into Callie's name the minute Dad died."

"But Callie is in a home," my daughter started.

"Yes, and now her daughter, Carlyn, is going to do what she has to do."

"They could have at least waited until Grandpa was in the ground." My daughter smacked a hand down on the table. "Carlyn can't wait to get her mitts on everything here!"

"People aren't always kind," I told her.

"Boy, if Grandpa knew he would be mad!"

"I think that he does know," I said in almost a whisper.

The following day was one of hectic events. Funeral planning is not easy and it gets more involved with time.

I was on the phone when Karen came out of the restroom. Her blond hair was hanging loose around her face. It gave her an even taller look than the five-feet-six she stood.

"What were you doing in Grandpa's room last night?" she asked me.

"I wasn't doing anything in Grandpa's room. Why?"

"What was all of that noise then?"

"What noise?" I asked.

"Well, I don't know, Mom! I thought it was you sorting through things!" She stood in thought for a quick minute and then said, "It was a weird kind of noise—like wind was trapped in that room or something. Like a cyclone was trapped in the room. Heck, I don't know"

"Let's go look."

"What?"

"Let's go look into the room together and see what the noise was," I said softly.

Grabbing the key from the key holder, I inched toward the door.

My daughter reached out and grabbed my hand. Her eyes looked deeply into mine and she said, "Has this door been locked since you found Grandpa?"

"Yes," I said.

"Then, how?"

By now I was at the door and opening it. The room was a total shambles. Papers, clothes, shoes, and other things looked as if they had been tossed around the room by a strong wind. Well, Karen had said it sounded like a wind had been in there.

"Mom," Karen said behind me. "You mean this door was always locked?"

Walking around the room, we saw that all of the windows were shut. All of them, except the window looking into the garage, were locked tightly on the inside. This, as well as the musty smell of the room, told us that the windows had not been opened in several days (if not longer) and no wind had been in this room.

"This is freaky, Mom." My daughter bustled into the kitchen and flopped down in a chair.

After looking around Dad's bedroom one more time, I pulled the door closed. This time I decided not to lock it. The damage of this room had already been done to me. Not only had I lost my father, but I was also being forced to move out of the house that had been my home for the last few years. The house that I was to receive for giving up years of my life to take care of my father and his second wife would no longer be my home.

"Look, Mom," Karen said as she pointed to the clock on the wall. The clock had turned upside down! For twenty years, that clock hadn't moved (the dust proved it) and now—in the last few minutes—not only had the clock turned upside down unassisted, but dust was sprinkled on the carpet beneath the timepiece.

"What is going on here?"

"I'm scared, Mom." Karen suddenly looked very young to me, and her bottom lip quivered. In the distance of the confines of the house, we could hear a wind picking up in Dad's room. It sounded like a hurricane.

Fixing the clock, I went back to the room and threw open the door.

"What is going on here?" I said, but everything in the room was still and just as I had left it. Karen, eyes wide in terror, looked into the room from beside me.

"What does it mean, Mom?" she almost whispered.

"I think I know," I said suddenly and we both returned to the kitchen.

The clock was upside down again and anger shot through me, jolting through my arms and into my hands. I fixed the clock again and almost yelled, "That's enough, Dad! That is just enough! It doesn't matter what you do, or how much you destroy—Carlyn still gets this house and I am out! And—dammit—I'm too tired for this!"

The house was quiet.

The clock was straight on the wall and the wind in the bedroom was gone.

Though things were depressing for me for quite a while after that, I have learned that all things happen for a reason. Carlyn didn't end up getting the house or the furnishings. All those items had to be auctioned off to pay for the care center bills for her mother. You see, Callie lingered on for a year or two after that. Carlyn didn't have to tell me to get out in two weeks, but it was probably better that she did. I was still sad about my father, which limited the amount of self-pity I could feel.

Many other things have happened that lead me to believe that my father's spirit has hung around to keep an eye on things and on me. Every once in a while, I can feel a large hand on my shoulder, but when I turn to look, no one is there. Sometimes, I can hear a voice in the rushing wind. It seems to tell me that everything will be OK.

Born Christina Louise Havlatko in Long Island, New York, on May 7, 1957, Christina grew up in the lower west side of Cleveland, Ohio. In 1973, she dropped out of high school and married. After the birth of her only child, Karen Anne, in 1974, Christina decided to gain her General Equivalency Diploma and become a writer. Her first story was published in 1980, and she also passed her GED test that year.

In December 1983, Christina's story "Dreams & Fantasies," was dramatized by the American Cancer Society and presented as a musical at the Cambridge Performing Arts Center in Cambridge, Ohio.

Pan's 25th Horror Collection (London, UK) in late 1984 contained a short story by Christina titled "Grave Business." Most exciting was that the volume also contained a story by Stephen King. The twenty-fifth edition was also the final edition to be edited by celebrated writer and editor Herbert van Thal.

As Christina Kiplinger-Johns, she has seen over six hundred pieces of her work published. She's listed with Poets & Writers, Inc. Her biography is included in *Who's Who in the Midwest* and she is listed in *International Authors* and *Writers Who's Who* (London, UK). She was also listed as a Distinguished American two years in a row by the American Biographical Institute.

Her first poetry book, co-authored with Maria Alexander and titled *Biting Midnight*, was published in 2002 by Medium Rare Books. Still in Ohio, Christina has four grandsons who share her love of horror. Her web presence is http://www.bloodredpens.us.

From the Beyond

by Anne Whitaker

"You must go on holiday. Of course you must."

My eighty-three-year-old mother-in-law was in hospital following a mild stroke. She was in London, England; we live in Glasgow, Scotland, four hundred miles away. We were exhausted; 1999 had been a year of seemingly unremitting family problems, ill and dying friends, and work stress. Our holiday to the island of Madeira had been booked for a couple of months—looking forward to it was the only thing keeping us sane. With a week to go before we set off, Barbara had been taken to hospital.

We agonized. Should we cancel our holiday and go to London? The medical staff had assured us Barbara was stable. My husband spoke to her; I spoke to her—there was no question in her mind. We badly needed our break. Of course we should go. We could pop down to London to see her on our return in two weeks.

It all seemed perfectly sensible. There was one problem, though. The tone of the words at the top of this page, the last words spoken to me by my mother-in-law before we set off for Madeira, haunted me all the way there. Why? The words were innocuous, but in the tone I caught a whisper of the beyond—that was the only way I could describe it to myself. It had made me shiver. Was she going to die?

I was born on the Celtic fringes of the British Isles—the island of Lewis in the Outer Hebrides. There is a long tradition there of what is known in Scotland as the second sight—a faculty of seeing the future, being able to see the spirits of the dead, and at times of knowing when people are going to die. My maternal grandmother had been known for possessing the sight. We never spoke of it, but my mother had it to a less marked degree. And the sight wisped in and out of my life: episodically, unbidden, unpredictable… and unwanted.

I did not want it now.

I said nothing to my husband, although I felt that we should have gone to his mother. Rejecting the sight in myself, I could not trust its wisdom, didn't know whether my intuition was the sight or my own melodramatic streak.

Madeira is a beautiful island. Settled in a wonderfully comfortable hotel, we set about exploring the island's majestic scenery and cultural richness. But I could not relax. Despite telling myself that Barbara was stable, comfortable, and well cared for, I continued to feel edgy and uneasy. Returning to the hotel on the third day of our holiday, after a day of exploring, I just knew a message from Ian's sister would be waiting. It was. Barbara was dead.

The next few days were a blur. Grief, shock, regret, the practical difficulty of cutting our holiday short to return home all created an emotional maelstrom that sucked us in. I can still clearly recall the first incident. Twenty-four hours after Barbara's death, as I stood just outside the french windows of our hotel room, seeking calm in the cool dampness of the grass under my bare feet, inhaling the evening fragrance of jasmine and hibiscus, the voice began.

"Annie. Annie!" There was a soundless insistent whisper just behind my right ear. I shook my head to clear it. I was overwrought; surely it was just my imagination. The voice persisted. I ignored it, went inside, and got changed for dinner. I said nothing to Ian.

The next day we went to evening service in Funchal cathedral, seeking comfort from the spiritual atmosphere that pervaded this place where so many had worshipped over centuries. We both believe that spirit is present in any sacred place, whether a Roman Catholic cathedral or a secluded grove of trees beside a remote stream high up in the hills. Besides, Barbara had been a deeply religious woman, and she would have liked the thought of us attending church to say prayers for her.

We were seated, watching as worshippers filed toward the priest to make their communion.

"Annie. Annie!" This time I felt rattled and a little alarmed. Was I hallucinating? Once again I mentally shoved the voice away. My rational side came up with explanations. It was my imagination. I was overwrought. But this time the voice would not be shoved away. It persisted. "Annie, please listen to me. I need you to give a message to Ian from me."

My late mother-in-law, an open-minded lady, had a dear friend living in the same retirement complex who was a spiritualist medium. Knowing that Barbara had accepted this side of Lady Jo's life as entirely valid, I had confided some of my own paranormal experiences, including one in which I had encountered an old lady on a train who had offered to teach me mediumship. Barbara knew that I had this "other" side. Was she using this knowledge to try and use me as a medium for herself?

"I don't want this. Please, please leave me alone." With an effort of will I distanced myself sufficiently to shut out the voice. Again, I said nothing to my husband, who in fact had more faith and trust in my other side than I had.

Intermittently over the next couple of days, the voice persisted. It simply would not leave me alone for long and kept repeating the same thing. A note of mild hysteria and bizarre humour began to creep into my reactions. I felt as though I was being persistently nagged from the other side!

Eventually, I gave in whilst walking up a fairly long and tiring hill in considerable heat toward our hotel for an early afternoon siesta. There was a low wall to our left and a busy road on our right.

"All right, all right! What is it? I'll tell him if you promise to go away and leave me in peace."

"Annie, I have never in Ian's whole life told him that I loved him. Please, will you tell him this from me?"

"But Ian knows very well that you loved him."

"I never said the words. Please, please, say the words for me and I will never trouble you again."

There in a dusty, hot, Funchal street, I told my husband what had been happening to me for days, and what his mother's message was. In the silence that followed, the voice came one last time—"Thank you"—and it was gone.

Whilst we were both digesting this experience in silence, an extraordinary thing happened. I still find it hard to describe, despite clear recall. Suddenly, following the silence after the "Thank you," there was a soundless babble inside my head accompanied by images of disembodied faces whose eyes seemed hungry for something from me. I had occasionally had these images before whilst falling asleep or waking up, but never before in the middle of a busy street in broad daylight. What did this feel like? It felt exactly as though the word had got around that there was an open channel, and a scramble of people was struggling each to get their own message through. My head began to spin so much that I became dizzy, stopped walking, and had to lean on the wall for support.

Something inside me found the mental strength to yell out soundlessly: "Get away from me! I don't want this! I don't want this!" Gradually, the babble subsided.

I was aware of Ian staring at me intently. "What on earth is wrong with you? You look as though you've seen a ghost!"

I told him what had happened. "Do you think I'm going mad?"

"No, but I do think you have to *do* something with this side of yourself one of these days." Slowly and silently, hand in hand, we walked back to the hotel. I felt exhausted, desolate, and empty. But it didn't feel like my desolation and emptiness....

Later that evening, over dinner, having rested and recovered somewhat, I asked my husband whether his mother had ever said out loud that she loved him.

"No," he replied. "She never did. Not until today."

Anne Whitaker lives in Glasgow, Scotland. She began a new career as a freelance writer in early 2004 after many years in higher education teaching, psychiatric social work, private counselling and supervision, and the teaching and practice of astrology. She holds a diploma from the Centre for Psychological Astrology in London, as well as an MA degree and postgraduate diplomas in education and social work from Scottish universities. She has had many articles, essays, and pieces of journalism published in recent years, including Scotland's award-winning *Sunday Herald* newspaper, *Kindred Spirit*," a well-known UK alternative magazine, and *The Mountain*

Astrologer and *Considerations* in the United States. Currently, her main writing themes are the paranormal, the midlife transition, happiness, the healing power of nature, and planetary cycles as an aid to personal growth. She is keenly interested in the developing relationship between cutting-edge physics and spirituality, and in the theory of reincarnation. Anne can be contacted by e-mail at a.whitaker@ecosse.net.

Last Words

by Beverly Forehand

My grandpa took a walk everyday at three o'clock in the afternoon. He called it his constitutional, and fair weather or foul he'd get out his hickory and cherry walking stick and set out across the fields. He liked to walk along the farm's perimeter to inspect the fences for wear and storm damage. Cows are sneaky creatures that would take even the slightest opportunity to make a run for it.

Sometimes, if I asked, he would take me with him on his walks. But, it was cold that day, a frosty day in November only a week before the first big snow, and I was already helping my grandmother in the kitchen. My granny was making teacakes and both she and I had dough up to our elbows when he left. We heard him say that he'd be back in a bit. We hardly looked up from rolling the vanilla-scented dough when he left.

We finished making the teacakes in about an hour. And, after eating two or three each, we decided to start a fire in the big wood stove my grandparents kept in their living room. Granny sent me out to get some kindling and a few sticks of wood. It took me a couple of trips since eight-year-old arms can't carry more than a stick or two at a time. I took my time getting the wood. Sometimes there were mice in the wood box and I was always leery about sticking my hand in it. I'd reached in and ended up with a handful of mouse more than once. I could see the first two pastures from the end of my grandparents' porch, but I couldn't see my grandpa anywhere. Usually, he was only gone half an hour or so. But I figured he was checking on one of the cows that was about to calve or that he might be in the barn.

We got the fire going and settled back to look through some old picture boxes. My grandmother must have had ten huge crumbling boxes of pictures. Each box was stuffed with photos of relatives in no particular order. I liked to sort through them all, asking who each one was and placing them in piles on the floor. I grabbed more teacakes and settled down by the pictures, expecting Grandpa to be back any minute. Granny told me to stop stuffing my face with teacakes and warned me that I was ruining my supper.

Granny didn't want to start dinner until Grandpa was back. If he was looking after one of the cows, it might be a long time before he came back up to the house and everything would be cold by then. I remember sitting on the wood floor sorting through the big box of pictures. Some of the pictures were so old that they flaked to bits when you picked them up and some were made of tin and had pictures of relatives that lived during the Civil War. I sat on the hard wooden floor, waiting and looking at those pictures. Teacake crumbs kept falling in the box, and I would have to stop and pick them out. I felt nervous, but I couldn't figure out why. Granny kept getting up every little bit and looking out the chintz dot curtains on the window above the door. She always kept the big iron key that opened the front door stuck in the keyhole and every time she looked out the window, the key would jangle and make a low rustling noise that sounded like someone trying to get in. Even though we had a fire going and Granny kept adding wood, the room was so cold.

Hours passed and Granny told me to go and call my dad to come over and look for Grandpa. Granny had a bad knee and couldn't walk very far over the uneven fields even with her cane.

She knew she'd never make it up to the far pasture where the cows liked to go when they were about to calve. I tried the phone, but it was busy. So I decided I'd just run down the road to my house and let my dad know that Grandpa was probably having trouble with one of the cows and Granny wanted to know if he could lend a hand. My dad was in the basement working on his truck when I got there. He said it might be a little while, but that as soon as he got the truck going he could come down and help Grandpa with the cows. I took off back to Granny's house, cutting across the creek. There was ice in places, so I had to be careful not to slip. I was so intent on watching my feet, I never looked up to the fields. I could have seen across them easily from the creek bank.

When I got back to my granny's house, she was sitting in her big, leather chair with the afghans wrapped around the arms, staring at the door. I told her that Dad was on the way in the truck, but she said Grandpa wasn't coming home. "What do you mean?" I asked her. I felt confused and started to cry for no reason.

And, she said, "Your grandpa's already been here to tell me not to worry and that he's all right, but he won't be coming home." I sat down in the floor then and started crying in earnest, because I knew she meant he was dead.

In about an hour, my dad came up to the house. He'd seen Grandpa sleeping against the fence post like he used to do sometimes on sunny days after he had taken his walk. Dad thought it was a little cold to be napping outdoors, but my grandpa always did exactly what he wanted to do. But when my father got up to him, he saw that my grandfather wasn't sleeping. The emergency room physician said he probably had a heart attack while he was sleeping. Granny told my dad not to worry, that Grandpa had said his last good-byes to her, and that she knew he was in a better place and that everything was fine. I just wish I had been there to see him one last time and to hear his last good-byes to us all.

Beverly Forehand is a freelance writer and painter living in Nashville, Tennessee. She has published several short stories, poems, and a pet cookbook. Her hobbies include cultivating her medieval herb garden and telling her cats (unsuccessfully) to stay off the couch.

A Little Change

by Candy Killion

My father was the quiet, studious type, the sort of guy whose idea of a good time was not making superficial small talk. Almost painfully shy, he spent a large portion of his leisure hours buried in one of his mountains of books, which were piled here, there and everywhere—from bedside to bathroom. Among the four or so concurrent reads he had going on any given day—jumping from the center of something by Salinger to the dog-eared beginnings of *The Complete Sherlock Holmes*—were also his numismatic price guides and the half-filled coin collector keepbooks that went with them.

Of all his reading rooms, the bathroom was his favorite. Our frantic and impatient pounding on the john door largely fell on deaf ears when Dad was immersed in checking out his latest double-die obverse. "Fine, fine, I'm getting out of here now!" His halfhearted stab at pretending to be annoyed would diffuse through the bathroom door, back-dropped by the jingle of wheat pennies and buffalo nickels and Mercury dimes tinkling and rolling on the cool tile floor.

"In a minute, in a minute!" We knew the drill, and we'd laugh nearly uncontrollably, crossing and uncrossing our legs to try to stop the call of nature as he flushed the toilet and mumbled under his breath, scooping coins up. Self-possessed and suddenly regal, he'd emerge from his throne room, coin books tucked safely under his arm, peering over his square-rimmed glasses. "We need more bathrooms!" A playful smirk would cross his face, his wide black eyebrows arching and nearly disappearing into the deep furrows of his brow.

My sister, Trish, would give him her best "harrumph," and shaking an impudent finger, toss back, "No, Dad—you need to use your desk!" Shoving past her, I'd usually claim first dibs to the toilet, to her chagrin.

After many of these frequent bathroom battles, she or I—depending upon who stayed behind to taunt our father—would generally emerge from his "library" with one of his absentmindedly forgotten treasures in our jeans pockets. "It's a Denver." I'd wander into Dad's den, where the old knotty pine desk sat, heaped with the read and unread, and with no open space for elbowroom. My father looked up from his chair over in the less-cluttered corner, and over his glasses again, his palm outstretched, as I plunked the tiny silver piece—tails up—into his leathery hand. "You left another one of your babies behind, Dad."

This time I'd said it, but the wisecrack was interchangeable between my sister and me.

My father would stop fiddling with the coins, resting his glasses atop his thick blue-black curls, and rub his eyes. And then he'd answer the same way he always did when the familiar barb flew. "You two are my babies. Don't be smart."

Trish and I would invariably throw an arm around his neck, then, and whisper, "Yeah, we might be your babies, but the coins are your best friends, Dad."

Night after night, Dad sat within earshot of us, examining the fine-lined wheat stalks, the curve of the bison's back, the crisp detail of a very fine caduceus. Night after night, he came home from work and put on what had been my mother's apron, setting dinner on the table within the hour, and checking our homework as we did the dishes afterward. And night after night we followed him from kitchen or bathroom to the den, where the same amiable teasing led us to his corner and the chair where he sat peering over his glasses, forever at work on his precious hobby, but also always comfortably and persistently within our reach.

Like most kids, it wasn't until our childhood was over that we came to grips with what exactly it was that made our father tick. Middle years to adolescence whizzed by as my sister and I continued to balk at Dad's habit and shake our heads at what we considered terribly wasted, lonely time, knowing, surely, he could have had better things to do.

Then, one day, when I was a freshman in college, Trish called my dorm. "If you can head home for a visit this weekend, it might be a good idea." She wasn't her usual bouncy self, and had no snappy comeback ready when I joked about how she needed to adjust to having a bedroom to herself, without me.

Trish stood grim-faced, arms folded, on the side porch of my father's tiny, white Cape Cod. "Shh!" She lifted a finger to her lips, and grabbing my arm, pulled me into the backyard.

"Something is wrong with him. He hasn't touched the coins. Not at all! All of a sudden, it's like he's a different person. It's—weird."

Sure enough, the piles of coins that were a collector's dream were nowhere in sight as I poked my head into Dad's den. I was taken aback by the sight of warm, polished pine and the smell of orange oil. It occurred to me I had never seen the top of his fine old desk. The piles and piles that had covered it were gone. "Don't just stand there—give me a hand taking these books up to the attic, will you?"

My father lay a hand on my shoulder, peering over his glasses like always, but looking somehow different. Thinner, perhaps.

"What's going on, Dad?"

"Not a thing, except a little change. You're off to school now; Trish will be right behind you. Time for me to get off my duff and do a little living, don't you think?"

My sister and I exchanged uncertain glances and helped him clean out the rest of the den.

A few more years passed. By now, both my sister and I had set up careers and our own households, but checked in with our father frequently. His den still smelled of orange oil and the desk remained uncluttered. Dad would never tell us why he suddenly stopped fiddling with his precious coins, even when pressed. "I had better things to do," he explained tersely.

He grew thinner and thinner, and the day came when Trish and I sat on the floor of his den amid boxes of books hauled from the attic, sifting through my father's things and trying to reassemble the pieces of the life he left behind. "I'll never understand, " I said quietly, "why he gave up the coins. He never told me. Did he tell you?"

"No," said Trish, fighting back tears, "but I think this may explain it." She held up a receipt lying atop a dusty box filled with empty coinkeepers, their thick blue cardboard covers no longer holding lovingly inserted tiny treasures. We read it together. What it told us was that he had turned in his collection when I went to college, sacrificing one love for another in financing my future.

The guilt I felt at depriving my father of his one dear pleasure just overwhelmed me. Going into his bathroom, I ran the cold water full-force and splashed my face. I looked at my reflection in the mirror over the sink, red-eyed and swollen, and spoke out loud: "Daddy, why?"

"Are you OK in there?" Trish knocked on the door, like we had when we were kids. "In a minute! In a minute!" Hearing my father's words coming from my mouth made us both laugh. As I opened the bathroom door, I caught the tiniest glimpse of something on the cool tile floor, and bent down to pick it up. It was a wheat penny, dated 1954. The year I was born. "Do you feel it?" Trish asked.

I did. As I gripped my penny from heaven in my hand, I felt a familiar hand on my shoulder, fully aware that from where my father sits now, no doubt surrounded by piles of buffalo nickels and Mercury dimes, the occasional wheat penny will cross my path and remind me we will always be his babies.

Candy Killion has been a freelance writer for more than thirty years, but "A Little Change" is her first exploration into the very real world of the afterlife. Most of her published work, as in the upcoming *Rocking Chair Reader* (Adams Media series), focuses on family interaction among the living. "The line," she says, "between us and them becomes fainter and fainter as I age. And now is the time to write about it."

She lives in southeast Florida with her husband, John, and a cat named Mouth who does all the things one of her sainted tabbies used to do. This mother of four and grandmother of three still feels her father—the focus of her story—nearby. His photograph hangs on the wall near her keyboard, very close to a handful of old pennies. Every now and then, she still feels the touch of a familiar hand on her shoulder. And, strangely enough, it doesn't give her the shivers. She can be reached through http://get.to/candykillion.

Karen Ann Carpenter is an extremely versatile writer. Her fiction can be charming, funny, scary, sensual, philosophical, or … gross! She'll take a break from writing a gruesome horror story to create a magical fairytale land for children—or to perfect an apple pie recipe for her holiday cooking newsletter, *Celebrate The Now*. Karen also writes non-fiction articles that highlight the eerie and mysterious possibilities of life. She lives in New Jersey with her husband, and their black Labrador retriever, Buddy. Visit Karen on the web at KarenAnnCarpenter.com.

Look for other titles from the Haunted Encounters series:

The Book That Started It All!

Haunted Encounters: Real-Life Stories of Supernatural Experiences

Real Stories. Real people. Real haunted encounters. Delve into authentic tales of the supernatural, as told by the people who lived them. Forty-six stories of the unknown; some will touch you, others will make you smile, and many will make you want to sleep with the lights on. In bookstores everywhere.

ISBN 0-9740394-0-3

An International Ghost Event

Haunted Encounters: Ghost Stories from Around the World

Authors from the far reaches of the globe combined for this anthology of real-life haunted encounters. You'll see that supernatural experiences span countries, races, religions, and cultures—and this group of authors prove it! Look for it in you favorite bookstore.

ISBN 0-9740394-1-1

The Most Unique Book of True Ghost Stories You've Ever Read!

Haunted Encounters: Personal Stories of Departed Pets

The deep bond between animals and humans has never been so well demonstrated as in the pages of these true accounts of ghostly encounters with beloved pets. Curl up with your favorite furry friends and enjoy this loving collection of interesting experiences by real people.

ISBN 0-9740394-2-X